The Urban University in America

The Urban University in America

Maurice R. Berube

GREENWOOD PRESS, INC.
WESTPORT, CONNECTICUT • LONDON, ENGLAND

Library of Congress Cataloging in Publication Data

Berube, Maurice R.
    The urban university in America.

    Bibliography: p.
    Includes index.
    1. Universities and colleges—United States.
2. Education, Urban—United States.   I. Title.
LB2328.4.B47   378.73   77-87917
ISBN 0-313-20031-9

Library of Congress Catalog Card Number: 77-87917
ISBN: 0-313-20031-9

First published in 1978

Greenwood Press, Inc.
51 Riverside Avenue, Westport, Connecticut 06880

Printed in the United States of America

10   9   8   7   6   5   4   3   2   1

378.73
B55 2u

193/53

K.D.

For
Emerilda Berube Ryan
and
Kathy Berube

Contents

Acknowledgments

I am indebted to a number of people in the preparation of this book. Dr. Marilyn Gittell of Brooklyn College, with whom I worked for a number of years and coauthored three books, was a prime influence. Dr. Gittell has been a singular force in urban affairs, being the first editor of *Urban Affairs Quarterly* and a founder of both the Institute for Community Studies and the Urban Studies Department at Queens College, City University of New York. She initiated my interest in the subject of the urban university in America, introduced me to the larger world of urban problems, and suggested pertinent ideas.

There were many others who helped in some fashion in this project, from librarians to graduate students in my education seminars. Especially instrumental was Dr. Rita Arditti of Union Graduate School, who furnished much needed encouragement. Of course, the contribution of my wife, Anne Clarke Berube, is immeasurable. My son Michael proved a competent proofreader, and my daughter Jean gave moral support.

The Urban University in America

The rise of the urban university

The urban university has become the dominant institution of higher learning in America. It has been called upon not only to educate a majority of college students in America, but to provide leadership to a nation of cities. Within a generation, it is expected that eight out of ten people will live in metropolitan areas. More and more youngsters will attend urban universities, especially in the near future, as rising costs impel city students to attend a local urban college. Central cities are beset with ever-mounting problems and look to the learning community to help in providing answers.

Yet, the urban university has still to realize its full potential in responding to the urban challenge. Although the concept of an urban university is in keeping with long-standing traditions in American higher education, particularly those of the land-grant university, there are major obstacles to the fulfillment of the urban university's purpose. Most of these obstacles derive from a historic agrarian myth that only recently shows signs of abating.

We officially became an urban nation only in 1920, when, for the first time, a majority of our citizens lived in urban centers; today, nearly three-fourths live in cities.[1] Concomitantly, the urban university has emerged in full force only during the twentieth century, as has mass higher education, which fully developed only within the last generation. The concept of a viable network of urban universities adequately serving American cities can be realized by an enlightened public policy. Surely what was done for an agrarian nation through the land-grant college can be done for an urbanized America through the urban university.

By the seventies, the urban university emerged in significance, accounting for the large majority of American college students.[2] But in the last two decades, the urban university has faced severe crises. The first crisis of the sixties, triggered by student and community pressures, concerned the lack of involvement—"relevance"—in the social affairs of the city. The urban university was viewed by student and community activists as being a part of the national urban problem rather than a part of the solution. Charges by these groups against public and private urban universities were mainly threefold: the urban universities were perceived as economic barriers to the urban poor and low-income students who sought college credentials for employment; they were accused of uprooting the urban poor in their college expansion; and they were perceived as props for the status quo in their delivery of urban policy studies to government and established institutions. Consequently, urban universities became the targets of student protest and confrontations with ghetto communities. Major urban universities had their isolation shattered. Berkeley, Columbia, Harvard, City University—these great centers of learning found themselves in an adversary position to their clients and to their communities.

The second crisis of the seventies was equally serious as urban universities began to adapt to the social needs of the cities: survival. The affluence of the sixties with nearly full employment and an expanding economy gave way to the retrenchment of the economy and concomitant shrinkage of public funds for education. The prospective end of World War II baby-boom college enrollments severely depressed the market for private urban universities. In addition, the rising college costs encouraged more youngsters to attend public rather than private universities. Government cutbacks in spending for education reduced the public urban university's scope.

Yet, the urban condition in America increasingly deteriorated. Consider New York City. More than 1 million of its 8 million people are welfare poor. Fully one-third of its million-plus public-school students are more than one year behind in reading. More than 1 million middle-class citizens left for the suburbs in the decade between 1960 and 1970. More than ½ million jobs have evaporated since the end of the sixties.[3] These urban problems have been compounded by the city's inability to generate sufficient revenue to pay for services, requiring a loan from the federal government so it could avoid bankruptcy. What is true of New York City is true, in varying degrees, of every major American city.

Beginning in the late sixties and following through the seventies, urban universities began to respond to the conditions of the cities and attempted, in various ways, to involve themselves in the problems of the cities.[4] Most urban university administrators had now considered such involvement a majority priority.[5] This involvement concerned three basic objectives: educating an urban poor, establishing good community relations, and developing urban research and related studies. However, by the mid-seventies, the universities' involvement still could not be considered extensive.

In the past generation, American higher education has been radically altered. That transformation has not been the conscious result of educational reform; it has been an accidental development, without plan or purpose, dependent on the subtle and complex forces of geography and economics. Much of the student protest movement of the sixties to restructure the American university simply missed the significance of this most potent metamorphosis. Few educational critics took note of the change. Rather, most concerned college activists debated other issues of varying weight: campus governance, the university as a servant of the warfare state, and the aim of education in a technocracy.

Meanwhile, American colleges and universities were becoming urban and public. The typical American university student now attends a public urban university. Today, the American university is urban, public, and financed by government; fifty years ago, the typical American university was rural, private, and financed by donations and tuition. Today, public colleges and universities, accounting for two-thirds of all colleges and universities, educate three-fourths of the student population; fifty years ago, private colleges and universities educated three-fifths of the student population.[6]

As the nation became urbanized after World War I, the urban university came into being. A survey of 178 colleges shortly before the turn of the century showed that four out of every ten students came from farms. By the middle twenties, urbanization began to make itself felt, so that 145 out of 913 colleges and universities were located in the city, and nationally four out of every ten students attended urban universities.[7] With the approach of the thirties, the shift was in full force; by 1928 more students who attended state land-grant colleges came from cities than from farms; nine cities could boast major municipal universities operated by city government, with New York being the first major city (1847) to possess a municipal university system. New York alone has over 300,000 students in urban institutions, as many students as were in all the nation's colleges in 1900; Los Angeles has 150,000; Chicago, 120,000; Philadelphia, 95,000; and Boston, an estimated 90,000. Moreover, these figures represent only students in universities in the central cities, ignoring the larger neo-urban institutions in the outlying suburbs.

Few fully grasped the implications of these developments. There was some mild interest after World War II. The Association of Urban Universities, formed in 1914, eventually disappeared by the mid-1960s without having made a significant contribution. Foundations and colleges held symposiums and conferences, many dull and listless, and published tame proceedings calling for more federal aid. By the end of the sixties, urban studies and urban institutes slowly began to appear.

The urban university has had to struggle against historical elitist conceptions of the university to gain its direction. These concepts stressed (and in some quarters still do stress) the "objective" scholarly purpose of universities and downgraded the service function. The true university, advocates of these concepts charged, had no claims except those of scholarship, teaching, and research without any need to relate these to practical concerns. Some further asserted that the urban university was the conserver of mankind's values with the sole responsibility of remaining detached and objective.

Surely the idea of an educated class was essentially selective. One need only consult Cardinal Newman on the idea of a university, a nineteenth-century distillation of the medieval and renaissance traditions in education, to realize that higher education was anti-democratic. Newman's dictum of knowledge as being "its own end" set the tone of the college as a breeding ground for the elite. Newman merely restated the classical concept of higher education. His university man was trained to be morally superior, which in the temporal dimension more often than not implied social and economic superiority as well. It was a sexist ideal also; there was by and large no room at the college for women. How could the poor be freed from the world of mundane wants to contemplate the beauty of truth?

What is questionable is not the fostering of a greater sensibility, but that this sensibility could only be encouraged and shared among the happy few confounds the modern temper. In effect, Newman's idea of a university provides intellectual stimulation and socialization for gentlemen, the inheritors of leisure. What Newman offered was a cloistered university giving the appearance of being the moral counterpoint to a degraded world. For example, one of Newman's American disciples, Jacques Barzun, in *The American University* bemoaned the service university since it "has capitulated to the world and must now be judged with it as unworthy."[8] The true mission of the American university, Barzun stated, is to offer the intellectual pleasures of medieval man: "To make the point perfectly clear," he wrote, "let me suggest that if students came from the world they know to a monastic university, full of learning, devotion to teaching, and visible sacrifice to both, they would regain their piety and accept the most arbitrary regimen without a murmur."[9] But Barzun's "humanism"—one whose guiding principle is exclusion—was not widely shared by educators and the client public. Yet, this nostalgia for the Newman university persists.

Nor did the next revolution in higher learning depart from elitism. By the end of the nineteenth century, the German system of graduate education, with its premium on research, encouraged yet another form of elitism. The German university's aim was more intellectual than that of turning out well-attuned gentlemen; it stressed the development of an academic elite. The German revolution in higher education led to the deification of research and created the modern scholar, the academic specialist. Again, the specialist was of the few and not the many. The university was an end in itself; the German model, in effect, proclaimed that the university *was* the faculty. It existed solely for the academic specialist wherein he could pursue his research. Students were necessary only insofar as they, in turn, took their place as academic specialists.

But the role of the American urban university, as chartered by the land-grant college, has been social. The land-grant college was the major breakthrough in the conception of the role of a university. In 1862, Congress passed and President Abraham Lincoln signed into law, during the darkest days of the Civil War, the Morrill Land Grant Act, which would ". . . teach such branches of learning as are related to agriculture and the mechanical arts. . . ."[10] The aim of the land-grant colleges was to shore up the agrarian economy. Young America was still an agrarian nation; most of its gross national product in the years before the Civil War was developed in agriculture.

When Lincoln signed the Morrill Act, partitioning land grants to the states to build colleges and universities for the support of agriculture, he revolutionized higher education, although few were aware of the consequences at the time. For one thing, the federal government's bold initiative established a national higher education policy, agrarian in thrust, although education constitutionally has been the province of the states. More important, the Morrill Act gave birth to the situation of a service university fulfilling a national purpose. Congressional representatives of each state received 30,000 acres of federal land to build an agricultural and mechanical arts college. The states responded by creating sixty-nine land-grant universities.

The land-grant college had been created at a propitious moment. Land was plentiful and Lincoln had just embarked on a national program of expansion with the Homestead Act and the law mandating construction of a national railroad. The Morrill Act was an educational complement to a national expansionist agrarian policy.

The American university not only has its precedent of university service, created by the land-grant movement, but a specific history of social involvement. Our best historian of American higher education, Frederick Rudolph, points out that during the Progressivist era, universities extended the concept of service into an activist one. As early as 1887, Smith College pioneered in college settlement in New York, working with the city's poor Jews and Catholics. The grand aim of Smith's Protestant students was no less than "to bring into close relations this class, who having received much are ready and eager to give of their best, and the other class, who in poverty, ignorance and degradation have yet a singular readiness to receive."[11] Much of the college settlement's work was pure paternalism by today's standards involving the Puritan virtues: the poor would be given public baths, hymn singing, and lessons in thrift. But much of the college settlement movement was also purely social. In Milwaukee, for instance, students brought social-organizing techniques to the poor.

The college-settlement movement grew. The universities of Chicago, Michigan, Northwestern, Wisconsin, and Harvard, and Butler and Vassar colleges were examples of the settlement experiments. The settlement approach blended cultural concerns, with scientific lectures, with practical elements such as dispensaries, diet counseling, and coal cooperatives. The settlement movement was founded on the assumption that the cities had not lived up to their potential and that reformers must take an active hand in seeing that they would do so.

Rudolph's historical precedent of activism suggests that our system of higher education responds to the most delicate of social proddings. When the temper of the times is conservative, the university buttresses the status quo; when the nation is more socially oriented, the university begins to look outward. What was true for the Progressive era held true for the sixties and the seventies.

The American urban university is unique; it is an addition to the Newmanian and German concepts of a university. Newman's classical idea of a university had little social purpose. Liberal education consisted of gentlemen pursuing knowledge for knowledge's sake, with the known side effect of it being a cultivation of understanding and compassion. Yet, Newman recalled Plato, for whom the higher learning was reserved for the "higher learners," men of intellect; as for the rest who had been weeded out, they could attend to lesser occupations. The German model also flourished in the rarified air of the academically brilliant, hermetically sealed world of professionalism and research. It was the American brand of university that finally offered a substantial variation: the university serving the public weal.

To be sure, the American urban university signifies more than a service station. It is a mansion with many rooms, and in fact, pursues all three ends: education in the liberal arts, academic professionalism, and public service. But the service aspect of the American

urban university distinguishes it from comparable European institutions.

The perennial debate in higher education emphasizes one of these
influences to the detriment of the other two. Newman classicists such
as Jacques Barzun and Robert Maynard Hutchins ridicule the service concept as a bastardization of the university. They claim
America has turned ivory towers into vulgar and immensely inferior vocational schools. Others, like Christopher Jencks and David
Riesman, influenced by German models, hailed the professionalism
of higher education to the detriment of the humanism of the college
and its social purpose. Champions of the American service contribution, such as Clark Kerr, almost exclusively heralded the new
American university as a servant of society. Therein lies the history
of American higher education.

The most accurate description of the American university to date
(of which the urban university is the most recent variant) has been
Clark Kerr's perception of a new American university. (Kerr's 1963
prognosis of a "second great transformation" in American higher
education that began after World War II optimistically foresaw the
final result by 1970.) He wrote in the now famous passage in *The
Uses of the University:*

> The university is being called upon to educate previously unimagined
> numbers of students; to respond to the expanding claims of national
> service; to merge its activities as never before; to adapt to and rechannel
> new intellectual currents. By the end of this period, there will be a truly
> American university, an institution not looking to other models but
> serving, itself, as a model for universities in other parts of the globe. . . .
> The university has become a prime instrument of national purpose.
> This is new. This is the essence of the transformation engulfing our
> universities.[12]

Kerr's definition of the American university—a multiversity or
federal-grant university—gave plausible explanation to much that
was happening on our campuses. Surely, the multiversity basically
represented the finished academic mold as heir to the American
land-grant college. Nevertheless, the process had not been completed. Students have redirected the shape and content of American

higher education, as have the minor continuing forces of federalization and professionalization.

Although the multiversity's dedication to national service is distinctly American pragmatism, one cannot be fully satisfied with Kerr's scenario. Kerr failed to grasp the social content of higher education. He approached his subject like a Yankee mercantilist; knowledge was an "industry" that accounted for nearly one-third of the gross national product. His critics quickly seized on this devolution of the service concept and aptly scored him for this approach.

More important, Kerr's version of "national purpose" left much to be desired. He simply interpreted *national purpose* to mean whatever policies a ruling establishment may pursue. Consequently, his multiversity would function passively as an instrument of those policies, rather than creatively, as he, himself, ambiguously advocated. In Kerr's day, those national policies were anti-egalitarian. The multiversity was handmaiden to the warfare state. Michigan State University adventured a counter-insurgency in Vietnam; American University promoted counter-insurgency in Latin America through Project Camelot. These policies uncritically extended the American colonialist arm. Furthermore, the network of university defense contracts James Ridgeway described in *The Closed Corporation* revealed how deep the multiversity was in debt to the policies of the warfare state. Although Kerr was prone to accept any national purpose, students and radical liberal professors were not. They were repelled by this version of the American university.

One asks: Should not the urban university serve the warfare state less and the welfare state more? Our urban universities, John Gardner observed, have done admirably in extending their assistance abroad but have not yet brought themselves to render the same service to the cities of which they are a part. One would think the question is redundant. For as the center of all learning—both humanistic and scientific—the university should improve the lot of man. Even the Newmanian monastic model can be considered, within its context, as directly serving society just as much as truth in the long run.

Kerr's establishmentarian impulses, however, were in character. His all-too-easy acceptance of other direction reflects the university's traditional habit of responding to society *first*. Just as in Kerr's day, the university responded to federal influence; it reacted to the more anti-establishment social impulses of radical students and faculty. To a great degree, the university as a societal institution passively mirrors the changes in that society.

Kerr's multiversity, of course, never existed quite as he envisioned it. The multiversity neglected its urban environment, and Kerr only belatedly updated his university concept into a model urban-grant university. But few educators remembered the latter portrait; most remembered the former. Kerr's multiversity was the focus of student protest with its impersonal mass education and its adherence to a dubious national foreign policy.

Still, the multiversity and the urban-grant university are in the land-grant, American-style university tradition, emphasizing equality. Unfortunately, the Morrill Act precedent stands as a lonely testimony to the official rhetoric of educational democracy. Most American urban universities, public and private, cling to more meritocratic assumptions, so they are victims of a profound cultural lag. Conceived as an agrarian institution, resembling European elitist models, and wrapped in a myth that questions whether the poor are educable, the urban university confronts a future that demands no less than a deep involvement in the social condition of a nation of cities, repositories of many of the poor. Once the myths are discarded, it may be able to meet these challenges on surer footing.

What is an urban university? The most recent book, written in the middle sixties, that sought to define the urban university was J. Martin Klotscke's *The Urban University and the Future of Our Cities*, published in 1966. For Klotscke, the urban university consisted of an institution that had mainly the happenstance of being located in the city. Klotscke offered a bland portrait of the urban university. It is an institution, he argued, composed mostly of lower working-class students, that does not dominate the cultural or economic life of the city but does offer the city the civil services of its continuing education facilities for adults. At best, Klotscke contended, the urban university should study the city.

Equally important, Klotscke's portrait downplayed the darker side of the urban university. Klotscke did not mention any adverse effects the urban university had in its relationship with its clientele, its neighbors, and the city. Although much of the turmoil erupted after his book was published, the seeds for future conflict had long been implanted. His discussion of the University of Chicago's expansion in the 1950s was, for example, unsympathetic to the fortunes of the neighboring poor community. In the end, his conception of the urban university proved singularly one-sided.

The only other book addressed to urban universities was written nearly fifty years ago by Parke Kolbe, *Urban Influences in Higher Education in England and the United States.* Kolbe assayed a definition of the newly emerging urban university that is much closer to the mark than Klotscke's. Urban universities, he suggested, do not merely happen to be located in the city; some that are located in the city are not true urban universities. The true urban university must address itself to serving its urban environment, specifically, mainly through urban studies and by offering equal opportunity either by free tuition or low-cost tuition. Kolbe thus deduced that only 34 of the 145 urban universities were "true urban universities," all of which, parenthetically, belonged to the Association of Urban Universities.[13]

Even Kolbe was unsure of the academic value of the urban university. The true urban university, he posited as the last characteristic, must have "maintenance *in spite of departure from academic tradition* of standards of the highest type" (emphasis added).[14] The implication was, of course, that urban studies, although a function of urban universities, are a devolution of the learning process.

These definitions fall short of appreciating the total impact of the urban university. As we shall see in Chapter 3, some urban universities do dominate their cities both financially and culturally. Moreover, they are far from objective and impartial actors. They are city powers in their own right and their policies affect people beyond their campuses, training the bureaucratic manpower that operates the city's vital organs: the teachers, police, social workers, and other sundry civil servants who determine the quality of city policies. The urban university controls economic opportunity to a large extent by determining who shall gain entrance into its ranks;

its real estate policies affect its neighboring communities and the city at large; and its urban research and urban studies have an impact on urban policy. In sum, the urban university is a busy player in the life of the city.

There can be no static definition of an urban university any more than there can be a static definition of an American university, or just a university. Universities have been defined by their functions, and these functions change as the demands of society change. The urban university, then, is an institution of higher learning with a special responsibility to meet urban needs.

An urban university is not only a center of learning that happens to be located in a city. That is its minimum requirement. It should be an institution developed specifically for the purpose of relating to the wide range of issues faced by cities and their communities in the last quarter of the twentieth century. Their learning community should comprise the entire population of the city. A prior commitment would be the development of programs for all segments of that population, encouraging an interchange of ideas between the deliverers of services and their clientele. The urban university's philosophy of education should be clearly broad based, assuming that such a center of higher education must be available to everyone in the city. Its faculty and staff must be committed to that basic principle. Its curriculum should be specifically geared to areas of major policy in the city—human resources, environmental design and ecology, transportation, health and hospital services, housing, and planning. Within these general areas of moral concern a true interdisciplinary approach can be developed. Clearly, the specialties in the various disciplines now prevalent in colleges and universities are limited. A sociologist who is not relating social theory to larger policy implications does not belong in the urban college.

The creation of urban colleges is an effort to develop a pertinent curriculum, which in this instance means a meaningful approach to the study of and ultimate resolution of deep-seated urban problems. Perhaps it is optimistic to assume that a concentration of energies and resources in the study of urban life will be an effective means for finding answers, but certainly our lack of attention to these needs has proved a serious shortcoming. The land-grant colleges spent several decades experimenting with their role as institutions of higher education in terms of curriculum and research as well as in their service role. Over a period, they were able to work out a reasonable position and a genuine contribution to the American farmer. There is no reason to assume that an urban college system could not be expected to produce similar results under somewhat similar arrangements.

An urban college system must, however, have its own base of development and the flexibility to be different. It should not expect to be modeled after any of the existing institutions. Its purpose and role must be distinctive; its course of study and methods should also be different. It should be a model of experimentation, concentrating on innovation in all of its aspects. Perhaps in recruitment of students some urban college would seek out older, experienced students who lack credentials but have a wealth of practical work experience; others should recruit younger students, forgoing high school diplomas as a requirement for admission. It may be that the urban college can or should reach into the secondary education area and combine college preparation with its other roles as the land-grant college did in its own area of growth.

The urban college should be able to develop something comparable to the agricultural experimentation idea—centers of research and practical know-how serving city government, helping to supply city personnel, and encouraging them to develop new approaches to city problems. These centers can provide more effective in-service training on a regular basis to city bureaucracies. Hopefully, then, the special orientation and commitment to urban studies will make these colleges more effective and reliable centers for the purpose of serving city government than the colleges that now perform this role so poorly.

These colleges should be solidly based on the experiential learning concepts. Faculty and students should be running schools, building or renovating houses, developing plans, and working in hospitals or administering community health centers. These enterprises can be conducted jointly with the city or private industry or they can be independent laboratories for improving procedures and techniques. This direct involvement is an essential part of the role of an urban college, which should be committed to a realistic appraisal of urban needs and effective responses. An interchange of faculty and student body with personnel in city agencies and practicing administrations as well as community groups is essential to its purpose. The underlying concept of the college would be a dedication to social change and the improvement of city living. The use of technology as a tool for change would also be primary orientation. The natural and physical sciences in the colleges would be directed toward these ends. Chemists, biologists, and physicists would be concerned with the city's environment, translating their special competence into means for dealing with air- and water-pollution problems.

The urban college, particularly in its research function, could serve as a community and/or city advocate, exposing problems and offering proven solutions for change. It could serve as the city's innovation center with constant attention to new ideas. Different urban colleges might, in fact, develop areas of special interest and competence. In Chicago, mass transportation might be an area of special concentration; in New York City, education and teacher training; in St. Louis, public health; and so on. Students and faculty would be interchanged to develop experience in centers of interest. City personnel from around the country could be sent on leave for special training in these centers. The potential for development would be enormous if the investment and commitment were sufficient.

The urban college system should have provision for residence as well as commuter education, allowing for intercity exchange of students and staff. There can be no thought of using existing institutions. The urban college system should be a new category of higher learning, a new option in the diversified system already so much a part of the American system of higher education.

In sum, the urban college and university has great potential in playing an increasingly important role in the life of the city. But its future development depends, to a large extent, on educational policies that are fashioned in Washington. Although education constitutionally is the responsibility of the states, a strong federal hand is needed from time to time to establish national priorities. The federal involvement of a century ago in creating the land-grant college should be repeated with the urban university.

NOTES

1. Irene B. Taeuber, "The Changing Distribution of the Population of the United States in the Twentieth Century," *Urban Studies*, ed. Louis K. Loewenstein (New York: Free Press, 1977), p. 24.

2. Carnegie Commission on Higher Education, *The Campus and the City* (New York: McGraw-Hill, 1972), p. 25.

3. Jason Epstein, "The Last Days of New York," *New York Review of Books*, February 19, 1976, p. 17.

4. George Nash, *The University and the City: Eight Cases of Involvement* (New York: McGraw-Hill, 1973).

5. Martin D. Jenkins and Bernard H. Reis, "The Urban Involvement of Higher Education: An Analysis of Selected Trends and Issues," *Journal of Higher Education* XVII, no. 4 (July-August): 401.

6. J. Martin Klotscke, *The Urban University and the Future of Our Cities* (New York: Harper & Row, 1966), p. 88.

7. Parke Kolbe, *Urban Influences in Higher Education in England and the United States* (New York: Macmillan, 1928), p. 112.

8. Jacques Barzun, *The American University* (New York: Harper & Row, 1968), p. 208.

9. Ibid.

10. Edward Danforth Eddy, Jr., *Colleges for Our Land and Time: The Land-Grant Idea in American Education* (New York: Harper & Brothers, 1957), p. 33.

11. Frederic Rudolph, *The American College and University* (New York: Knopf, 1962), p. 367.

12. Clark Kerr, *The Uses of the University* (New York: Harper & Row, 1966), p. 86.

13. Kolbe, *Urban Influences*, p. 112.

14. Ibid., p. 196.

CHAPTER 2

The search for equality

American higher education has struggled with the question of who should go to college. As Professor Daniel Bell has observed, the idea of equality was never clearly defined in America. Consequently, two traditions of equality affecting higher education developed: one emphasizing meritocracy and equality of opportunity for those most intellectually able and another emphasizing opportunity for all, regardless of intellectual merit.

Historically, college was intended as the preserve of an elite. That elite, often class-based in the nineteenth century, did not necessarily have to show merit. College faculties emphasized character, and they would educate the sons and daughters of the rich into good citizens without undue concern for academic potential. The poor were something else. To qualify for a college education, they had to show merit. Thus, in the early nineteenth century, American college administrators devised the scholarship scheme—for bright, poor youngsters—as a means of entering the privileged academic groves. Later, education societies took up the slack, when colleges were financially pinched, by awarding support to promising young men of "talent."[1] But the not-so-bright poor were excluded from this Calvinistic elect until the emergence of the public land-grant colleges.

Meritocracy has one of its most influential advocates in Thomas Jefferson, who argued for his famous "aristocracy of talent." The idea was to nurture a society where the best and the brightest prevailed. In theory, the just society was considered one where equality of opportunity flourished so those with the most ability would rise to the top.

18

The proponents of meritocracy persevere. Perhaps the most articulate proponent, Daniel Bell, has made meritocracy a subtle and persuasive argument. Bell and others borrowed the phrase "meritocracy" from British sociologist Michael Young. In 1958, Young's *The Rise of the Meritocracy* was published, satirizing the close, competitive, modern society whereby "intelligence and effort together make up merit."[2] Bell perceived this notion to be in the American tradition and that the key to it was the IQ. "In the nature of meritocracy," he wrote in *The Coming of Post-Industrial Society*, "as it has been traditionally conceived, what is central to the assessment of a person is the assumed relation of achievement to intelligence, and of intelligence to its measurement on the Intelligence Quotient scale."[3]

For Bell, meritocracy is most just; it is "the displacement of one principle of stratification by another, of achievement for ascription."[4] What is essential to a rise of meritocracy is equality of opportunity, which Bell assumes. Equality of opportunity denies all influences for advancement save "fair competition open equally to talent and ambition."[5] Meritocracy based on equality of opportunity thus constituted the just society.

But the meritocratic conception of education only superficially appears socially just. In reality it most resembles the harsh Calvinism of our Puritan forebears, which sanctified the status quo: the gifted and well-to-do who succeed possess an inner grace, whereas the less gifted and less affluent who fail were destined to do so. By not helping the least able, meritocracy merely sanctions the results of a race that was fixed to begin with.

Moreover, life fails to conform to meritocracy. Reality does not follow so orderly a design as is found in Bell's philosophy. Economists Samuel Bowles and Herbert Gintis, for example, maintained that there is extensive evidence "that IQ is not an important determinant of individual economic success."[6] One study of executives discovered that those with mediocre college records earned $25,000 *more* annually than did managers with superior college grades.[7] The discrepency between IQ and success cannot be attributed solely to a lack of effort—the other part of the meritocratic equation. There are other factors in success not measurable by academic testing. Surely luck and timeliness have an important bearing on success;

being the right person with the right idea at the right time is crucial. Skills not susceptible to academic measurement contribute to worldly success. Personality, for example, having little to do with IQ, often determines career outcomes. Moreover, there are factors connected with the social system: inherited wealth and connections, discrimination, and the class structure in America.

Meritocracy holds sway, however, in the academic world of which Bell is a prominent member. Academic grades determine initial job success; the intelligence, tested and culturally measured, to manipulate abstractions is important for later academic success. But, in the larger world, other forces come into play.

There are other flaws to the argument on meritocracy. Bell and his colleagues, for example, assumed that the social system is intrinsically capable of providing equality of opportunity, necessary for the rise of a meritocracy. This contradicts the historical evidence of ethnic and racial discrimination in every facet of American life, including higher education. Bright Jewish students, for example (of which Bell was one), were systematically excluded from prestigious colleges and medical schools, even when they could pay, until the last generation. Many were able to go to college only at the first, free urban university, City University of New York.

The danger in meritocracy is that all the advantages are reserved for those who flourish in the classroom. The mediocre student is relegated to a secondary position. But by grooming only school achievers, and early ones at that, one may be making a costly mistake. Some of our great political figures, thinkers, artists, and poets did not necessarily distinguish themselves at school. Karl Marx, for example, showed little promise in history in his early years.

What of the not-so-intellectually endowed? Another academic tradition was developed that sought to advance those not of a meritocractic elite. The land-grant movement in the mid-nineteenth century opened its doors, albeit out of necessity, to all those, including the not-so-academically endowed, who wanted entrance. Our best historian of the land-grant movement, Edward Danforth Eddy, Jr., described the process:

The "matter of expediency" forced the colleges to forego entrance requirements. A few required part of a high-school course before the student could enter "the college." Most admitted the students directly from the common schools. Some went as far as the University of Missouri, which in 1891 allowed any student to enter provided he made application and paid a fee. The situation was the result of conflicting desires. On the one hand, the colleges were determined to serve the people, which meant taking students at whatever level they could find them. On the other hand, the colleges wanted desperately to be "institutions of higher education" but they realized that this was impossible if they were to be true to their heritage of the democratic tradition. Entrance requirements were raised slowly, but it was not until approximately 1913 that a majority would require a full high-school course. In addition to the lack of high schools, the colleges found the work of the existing schools inadequate and often inferior. The level of college work varied widely. Some institutions maintained what would not be considered a technical high-school course of study. Others attempted strong four-year courses. It would be some years before standards had become uniform and interchange of students was possible.[8]

The land-grant experiment with open admissions was repeated, to a certain extent, nearly a century later. The GI Bill of Rights provided the stimulus to mass education under lowered admissions standards. In 1947, twice as many students went to college as in the previous decade. Of these nearly 2.5 million students, slightly under half (49.2 percent) attended under the GI bill.[9] Not only were admission standards relaxed for these veterans, but they received preferential treatment in being admitted. A historical analysis of the GI bill revealed that "almost all colleges and universities modified their admission policies" for World War II veterans.[10] In addition, such special consideration was given veterans as admitting them without high school diplomas on the basis of examinations and providing remedial services on campuses for those with serious academic deficiencies. Nevertheless, studies have shown that these veterans proved academically superior to non-veterans even though "the mean high school average . . . of the non-veterans exceeded that of the veterans."[11] Chief reasons for this academic success were attributed to the age and maturity of the veterans along with their strong motivation.

A generation later, blacks and Puerto Ricans in New York City were to reassert this egalitarian tradition by demanding open admissions to City University. The chief spokesman for meritocracy,

Daniel Bell, characterized this latter thrust as raising the "demand for greater 'equality,' as a defense against being excluded," and thus creating an "issue of meritocracy versus equality."[12]

Bell was correct in perceiving the conflict between both traditions. An advocate of open admissions, Jerome Karabel, noted that open admissions "carries within it the seeds of an attack on meritocracy."[13] When everyone becomes entitled to higher education, regardless of merit, the rigid stratified society of meritocracy loses its impact. Moreover, the university as the chief determinant of a meritocracy becomes revolutionized. "Universal open admissions, however," Karabel concluded, "would destroy the close articulation between the meritocracy and the system of higher education."[14] Indeed, universal higher education strips the meritocracy legacy and renders it obsolete.

Much of the controversy over affirmative action programs at universities that admit minority students, especially at crowded medical schools, with less academic background than white, middle-class students, revolves around meritocracy. Proponents of affirmative action argue that other values besides intelligence should become criteria in admissions: an attempt to redress past social wrongs or an attempt to place needed minority graduates of medical schools, say, in neglected areas. On the other hand, the bright, white applicant has felt that his meritocratic concept of equality has been violated and sees himself as a victim of reverse discrimination. Throughout this controversy, administrators of prestigious colleges admit wealthy students without special academic merit with an eye toward eventual alumni contributions. The obvious solution, of course, is to admit everyone, but in the real competitive world, such as in medicine, scarcity fuels the false conflict over who is more equal.

Nonetheless, mass education has arrived in the last generation. Today, the United States stands alone in number of students admitted to college, producing the largest percentage who graduate from high school (75 percent), the largest percentage who attend colleges (39 percent), and the largest percentage who graduate (18 percent). The nearest rivals are Japan (11 percent who graduate from college), and the Soviet Union (9 percent).[15]

Understandably, those most excluded from college have been the poor. The historical evidence is sketchy but points to the conclusion that the poor constituted the group least likely to attend college. One reason for this in the early nineteenth century was the general disinterest in college by the population that suspected higher learning. Nonetheless, few youngsters at that time even attended common school.[16] By the latter part of the nineteenth century, college was viewed as a sanctuary of the elite by such organizations as the Knights of Labor, which labeled the college "the stronghold of privilege and anti-unionism."[17]

Prestigious colleges reserved some admissions for bright "charity" or scholarship students. By the early nineteenth century, new "provincial" colleges in New England were recruiting "pauper" scholars. David Allmendinger, Jr., showed that as many as one-fourth of the New England college population was made up of these "pauper" scholars. This figure was based on counting the number of older, mature students and examining the aid arrangements of such philanthropic organizations as the American Education Society. Allmendinger reported that the American Education Society, at its height in 1838, financially helped with differing amounts of aid as many as 1,000 of the some 4,000 to 5,000 students in New England colleges.[18]

The absolute numbers of both those going to college, as well as the "charity" students, were small, as was the percentage of college-aid people enrolled in institutions of higher learning—less than 2 percent. Equally important, college was not widely perceived as a means of social and economic mobility in the early nineteenth century. College could only guarantee pauper scholars employment in the ministry and teaching, which Allmendinger thought provided "no great material reward."[19]

Initially, the urban university was an upper-class and later a middle-class institution. The first free, public, municipal university, City College of New York, for example, extended educational opportunities to the emerging urban middle class. Most of the city's nineteenth-century students were the sons of middle-class merchants, grocers, carpenters, physicians, lawyers, and so on; in the first few years, the largest occupational group of fathers was that of the merchant.[20] One year before the founding of City College, out of a New York City population of ½ million, the only two colleges —and private at that—enrolled a grand total of 247 students.[21]

Certainly, many of the presidents of the elite colleges were not interested in social mobility. Harvard's President Charles Eliot, for example, felt that the carpenter's son should be a carpenter, and higher education was not meant for him.[22] Some sentiment existed to create people's colleges that would "teach the children of the poor to rise by their wisdom and merit into stations hitherto occupied by the rich."[23] But for the most part, America was not prepared to provide its urban citizens with the university opportunities it could offer its agricultural residents.

The dominant urban university, privately owned and controlled, sanctified meritocracy. Only the affluent could afford to attend college, save the bright "charity students" on scholarship. Moreover, private universities strongly resisted the land-grant movement, mostly out of resentment of being left out of state and federal funding; Harvard's President Eliot roundly condemned the arrangement.[24]

But the land-grant movement did not result in mass education. By the end of the nineteenth century, land-grant college students numbered slightly over 20,000.[25] The interest in schooling came largely in the twentieth century with industry and urbanization. Nevertheless, what evidence exists shows that the urban poor in large numbers were not substantially represented in colleges except in such schools as the free urban college in New York.

One reason the urban universities never educated the mass of urban poor was that the public schools also failed in this respect. Both the public-school movement in the 1800s and the urban universities, which took on form with the urbanization of the 1920s, did not directly administer to the clientele they were intended to serve. The public schools and the public municipal universities became the vehicles of social mobility largely for a working and middle class; neither the working poor nor later a welfare poor were able to take advantage of these free schools. Colin Greer in *The Great School Legend* adduced evidence to show that the poor failed in massive numbers in the public schools in the early decades of the twentieth century. By and large, the overwhelming majority of the poor were not educated in the public schools; they either failed or dropped out to work in an economy with many job openings for the dropout. Consequently, it was the rare poor youngster who went on to City College.

There was a striking irony to this development. Initially, the free, common-school movement began in urban centers in the northeast before the Civil War; yet, the land-grant movement was strongest in the middle west.[26] Consequently, there was little direct relation between the urban common school and the urban private university, and the western private academy and the land-grant college. But the common-school movement grew so that by the end of the nineteenth century over 40 percent of college students came from public schools. Nevertheless, as educational historian Lawrence Cremins notes, the public-school movement still favored the affluent over the poor so it never fulfilled its high aims. The urban, public high school student who went on to the private urban university was primarily middle class. By the first decades of the twentieth century, approximately 5 percent of New York City's ¾ million pupils in public schools would attend high school.[27] Many who dropped out —an estimated two-thirds—did so to work, leaving college as an option mainly for the well-to-do. A common complaint of educational reformers such as George Counts was that the public high school, intended for the poor, helped mainly the affluent.

One can graphically conceive of how universities educated the poor and lower working class by a rare study conducted by Ora Reynolds in the middle twenties. Reynolds sampled a cross section of colleges and universities—urban, rural, public, and private— and his findings starkly indicate that higher education catered to an upper and middle class. Three of every four fathers of college students Reynolds surveyed were from the staunch bourgeois fields of proprietorship, professional and managerial occupations, and agriculture. Twenty-eight percent had attended college (today, three out of five students are the first in their families to do so). The median income of the students' fathers was slightly over $3,000 and less than 3 percent of the students' fathers earned less than $1,000, all of which indicated how few of the lower working class and the poor were able to attend college.[28]

Some of the incomes of the parents of students in private colleges were staggering, even by today's income standards. Nearly half of the parents of students at Yale (47 percent), 55 percent of those at Washington and Lee, and 68 percent of those at Williams earned upwards of $10,000. An income of $10,000 in 1926 signified affluence.[29] One can see how private colleges and universities further stratified society.

Today, with under half of all college-age youngsters in institutions of higher learning, the poor are still least able to attend college. Samuel Bowles and Herbert Gintis reported that "the probability of a high school graduate attending college is just as dependent on parental socio-economic status as it was thirty years ago."[30] Indeed, those welfare poor whose family incomes were less than $4,000 in 1974 (the latest date for such figures) accounted for only 6 percent of the college population, with half of them in four-year colleges. What is of special interest is that students from lower middle-class families, presumably working class, dropped by half during the period from 1966 to 1974, whereas students from affluent families doubled in attendance.[31] By contrast, the Soviet Union graduates 80 percent of its professionals from low-income families.[32]

Few public urban universities have succeeded in grappling with the problem of educating the urban poor. A major study of accessible higher education, Warren Willingham's *Free-access Higher Education*, disclosed a haphazard educational pattern that unconsciously neglected the urban poor. Approximately three-fourths of our major urban centers are markedly lacking in available colleges and universities that provide a measure of *free access*, defined as institutions where it is relatively easy to be admitted and that maintain free or low-cost tuition. More than 100 major cities have no free-access college. Moreover, blacks are geographically removed from nearby free-access colleges.

This educational urban neglect is even pronounced in the two most education-minded states in the nation, New York and California. In New York, which has the most colleges, two out of three colleges are private institutions; of 34 defined as free-access institutions, nearly all are public community colleges. In California, the pattern is the same. Almost all free-access institutions are public community colleges—86 of the total 187 colleges in the state—

since only the top third high school graduates can be admitted to the senior colleges. The senior institutions, because of lack of facilities, were rejecting some nine out of ten applicants for admission. Also, the community colleges are not located where they would be most advantageous to the urban populations; in Los Angeles, for example, substantially fewer blacks than whites live near a community college.[33]

In time, this negligence was bound to cause severe repercussion to the urban university. By the end of the 1960s, students, mostly black, protested at innumerable urban universities such as City College, San Francisco State College, and Brandeis University. They demanded equality in urban universities. A major study of campus protests showed that one-third of all demonstrations were at urban universities in large cities with substantial poor, black populations. Moreover, one-fourth of all protestors' demands were for admitting more black students.[34]

A prime factor that has kept the urban poor out of urban universities has been a stringent admissions policy. Since World War II and the pressure for mass education, colleges have strengthened their admissions requirements. College administrators of both public and private universities have felt, correctly, that they were in a seller's market. Consequently, they introduced the theory of selective admissions: out of the mass of applicants one could pick and choose an academic elite. College administrators then made it increasingly difficult for a high school student to get into college. For example, in order for a poor youngster (before open admissions) from New York City to qualify for admission to City College, he had to obtain an 85 percent scholastic average for admissions in his high school combined with a high test score from a specially designed aptitude test. In 1924, that high school average was only 72 percent; in 1936, 78 percent; in 1962, 82 percent; by the end of the 1960s, it was 85 percent.[35] It has been the poor, particularly the black and Puerto Rican poor, that have suffered most from selective admissions.

The assumptions of selective admissions are deceptively simple. Once one accepts the argument of an inability to educate all who apply—on the grounds that the educational plant is lacking—the

job is to choose those applicants most likely to succeed in college.
So admissions policies are generally predicated on high school performance plus additional aptitude tests that serve to verify that
performance. This circular reasoning serves admission people
well: one expects students admitted to succeed in college; these
expectations influence that success; and that success confirms one's
expectations.

The key to admissions has been the aptitude tests. Since 1900
when it was first organized, the College Entrance Examination
Board has wielded increasing influence through administering aptitude tests for aspiring college students. The impetus to the board
were the eastern prestigious colleges that, according to one critic,
had more interest in "attracting to their own campuses the most
able students than in providing equal opportunity generally, more
to do . . . with organizing a 'meritocracy' than with anything else."[36]
The predictive value of the aptitude tests of college performances
made them popular. The end result was that the "College Board has
helped to perpetuate a class-based, meritocratically legitimated system of stratification."[37]

However, the doctrine of selective admissions has been far from
infallible. National studies on student achievement have shown a
student's college performance to be an extension of his high school
performance, so one can expect any high school graduate to survive college. An important study by Professor Robert Williams of
"high-risk" students and of programs for students in the 1960s
who were poor showed that those students were as likely to make
it in college as their more affluent counterparts. Williams estimated
that at least half of the nation's colleges and universities operated
some form of program for children of the poor. (None, however,
made strenuous effort to recruit students with severe learning problems.) The ingredients for academic success of the students in these
programs transcended traditional admission requirements. Among
the criteria Professor Williams suggested were such elusive quali-
ties of student learning potential as "minimal perception of self-
worth, emotional toughness, intense motivation to improve one's
life and success in some activity other than scholastic which requires
some sustained effort."[38]

There are limitations to the considerable number of academic studies emphasizing the impact of class on student achievement. A review of academic studies on class and student performance does conclude that background appears to be an influence in achievement but adds that class plays a much less important role than most scholars admit. For one thing, a highly intelligent young person has a good chance of attending college (on the other hand, if he is rich and of moderate ability, the student has an excellent chance of admission to college). Moreover, the influence of a student's social and economic background diminishes substantially in college years.

Another study reinforced the concept that social class is not necessarily the best predicator of college performance. Of 1,700 high school graduates followed through from 1966 to 1968 in two-year and four-year institutions, most responded to factors of high school program and self-image. The study concluded that dropout "relates to personal characteristics such as motivation and intellectual commitment, and neither ability or social class, supplementary tutorial nor financial aid is likely to have much effect on it."[39] Dropout rate was also "strongly associated with low academic self-image and with poorer grades, both in high school and college."[40] On the other hand, "socio-economic variables were less important."[41]

The other factor providing an obstacle to poor and low-income students in the city has been, of course, cost. For private universities, the price for a college education including tuition and living expenses away from home averaged some $5,000 a year by 1976, with the elite universities going as high as $7,000 a year.[42] For public universities the total was some $2,800 a year. Those living at home were required to pay an average $600 a year to attend public universities.[43] For the welfare and working-class poor, private and public universities that were out of town were out of the question. Some measures were instituted to ease the plight of the poor and low-income student in the seventies. By 1972, the federal government had established need-based Basic Educational Opportunity Grants. Some states created programs for aid to low-income students, for example, New York in 1974 with its Tuition Assistance Program.

Ironically, the most substantive and symbolic student protest over admitting the urban poor was at City College, the first free municipal institution in America. In the spring of 1969, black and

Puerto Rican students made the idea of open admissions a household phrase by striking the school, closing the college, destroying property, causing a near race riot, and forcing the resignation of the college president. Their proposal asked that all black high school students be admitted to City College regardless of grades and aptitude tests. City College, like many other urban institutions, did not reflect the population pattern in the city and thus failed to educate the mass of the city's large urban poor. Only some 15 percent of the college's 20,000 students were black or Puerto Rican, whereas in the city high schools, these groups constituted 40 percent of the student body.[44] The progressive tightening of admissions to City College required an academic grade average of 83 with a high SAT score. Nevertheless, the administration of City University, which was quite liberal, envisioned an open-admissions policy by 1975, provided state funds were forthcoming as expected in the university's master plan; City University of New York (CUNY) Chancellor Albert Bowker had declared publicly the need for an "educational bill of rights" that hopefully would guarantee "a college education for all who seek it."[45] City College boasted both a politically liberal faculty and a long history of liberal and radical student activity.

California had adopted an open-admissions plan in 1960 whereby all high school graduates were admitted to the state university system. However, in the California plan, students were assigned either to senior or community colleges based on their high school grades. The net effect was to create a two-tracked system of public higher education with the most "heavily white and upper class" in the senior colleges and the community colleges populated by "minority and low income students."[46] The City College protest was of another order; the students wanted *all* high school graduates to be admitted to the college, regardless of grades.

The CCNY protest could not have been more ill-timed. New York City was still tending its wounds from the most racially polarizing event in its history—the New York school strikes of 1968. Then, the teacher's union, the United Federation of Teachers, closed the city's schools over a dispute with the experiment in black community control in the Ocean Hill-Brownsville section of Brooklyn. The school strikes had not only pitted white against black, but black against Jew. In a city with a large Jewish population, and a large Jewish teaching staff both in the public schools and the city colleges, black anti-Semitism could only serve to congeal fears that undoubtedly were class and economically based.

Moreover, the CCNY dispute occurred at the tail end of thousands of campus protests. The general reaction was one of a public desire for order, even if achieved by repressive means. More important, the CCNY protest occurred during the primary campaign for mayor. With the exception of novelist Norman Mailer, who campaigned in the Democratic party more in a radical "new politics" sense primarily to advance issues rather than his own candidacy, each candidate had to consider the political mood resulting from the school strike. One of the most popular mayors in New York, Mayor John Lindsay, was overnight castigated for siding with the blacks in the school-decentralization struggle. Consequently, the strike rendered exceedingly vulnerable and weak a man who was once considered unbeatable for reelection and as having national prospects for the presidency.

An administration-faculty committee approved an agreement with the students that raised more questions than it solved. The pact called for a dual-admissions policy whereby half of the 1970 freshman class would be accepted under prevailing admission requirements and the other half would be admitted from the eleven high schools in black ghettoes surrounding CCNY. The reasoning of both parties to the agreement, of course, assumed that there were *not* sufficient facilities to provide for open admissions. All of the mayoral candidates, excepting Mailer, roundly denounced the dual-admissions plan as reverse discrimination. Their rhetoric was sharp and attuned to the political mood of the city. One Puerto Rican candidate, Herman Badillo, equated the plan with the creation of "two separate and unequal colleges." Mayor Lindsay termed the plan both "unfair" and "impractical."[47]

The sentiments of these political leaders were reinforced by spokesmen for the larger white community. Although the *New York Times* deplored the special tragedy in the CCNY confrontations because the protesting students were in support of goals that had been part of the administrations of both the college and the

City University, the paper condemned the dual plan. Socialist newspaper columnist Michael Harrington bluntly outlined the political
repercussions of the pact:

> For one cannot tell the 50 percent of (mainly) white working class
> and lower middle class kids who will lose out if the plan is adopted that
> they are the ones who must pay the cost of abolishing poverty. That is
> obviously not fair and, more to the point, it is politically explosive.[48]

The majority of CCNY faculty concurred. Certainly, the college
teachers' union raised its voice against the plan. Only novelist-
candidate Norman Mailer—representing a minority of the CUNY
faculty—"reluctantly" endorsed the dual admissions plan as better
than no plan to alleviate social inequities.

The senate faculty rejected the dual-admissions plan. Instead,
they put forward a token suggestion admitting some 300 more
black and Puerto Rican students by the next academic year on a
trial basis. However, the dispute over the dual plan became moot
when the City University decided to accelerate its deadline on open
admissions.

The heat generated among the faculty, however, was not dis-
pelled. The CCNY incident crystallized faculty opposition to open
admissions. When Mayor Lindsay prepared a special campaign
white paper advocating open admissions, some of his liberal academic supporters—some of national reputation like foreign policy
critic Hans Morgenthau—succeeded in having such a plank
dropped from their endorsement of the mayor for fear of academic
blacklash.

The CCNY protest was archetypical of the urban university's
problems with an urban community. On the one hand, university
administrators emerged as liberal, willing to respond to the needs
of the students and the urban community; on the other hand, faculties emerged as conservative, unwilling to concede some change
that might imperil their professionalism. This pattern became fa-
miliar nationally. The Urban Research Corporation reported in
their study of student protests, for example, that only in less than
one-fifth of these protests did administrators refuse to negotiate
(and concomitantly, only 6 percent of student demands were la-

beled "non-negotiable").[49] Faculties at such places as CCNY and Cornell repudiated agreements reached by an administration and the students.

However, the CCNY incident also revealed a growing pattern of political reaction. President Richard Nixon was swayed from sponsoring proposals that would affect protesting students only by the strong opposition of his liberal secretary of Health, Education and Welfare, Robert Finch. According to the Urban Research Corporation's studies, no less than nine pieces of federal legislation were introduced to punish protestors, and some punitive legislation was enacted in eight states. Administrators took disciplinary and police action in 39 percent of the student protests for 1969.[50] Clearly, the prospects for significant change in the social role of the universities were politically damaged.

The CCNY protest underscored a simmering political dilemma. A black underclass demanded entry into colleges regardless of archaic admissions policies; yet, an academic class and a white middle class wanted to maintain the *status quo*. The CUNY administrators resolved the question of quotas by advancing their open-admissions policy, thus giving the mayor the political burden. He, in turn, while endorsing open admissions presented the governor and the state legislature, which paid half of CUNY bills, with the major responsibility.

The City College strike detonated strong political and academic counter-pressures even on the national political scene. Politically, open admissions encountered a powerful foe in the vice-president of the United States, Spiro Agnew, no doubt reflecting the sentiments of the administration, who denounced both open admissions and the quota system as perhaps "equally bad." The vice-president was explicit about his opinions on open admissions. "I do not accept," he said, "the proposition that every American boy and girl should go to a four-year college."[51]

The rallying cry of the academic opponents of open admissions became a supposed devolution of academic standards. Yet, these academics were unmindful of history. The GI Bill of Rights had flooded the higher education scene, shortly after World War II, and scores of students were admitted with no harm to the universities. On the basis of the GI Bill and the Morrill Act there was precious

little evidence to support the calamitous predictions of open-admissions opponents. The *Saturday Review* Education Supplement correctly diagnosed the new elements in the open-admissions debate
as race and poverty. "What is different about the current discussion
of college for everyone is, of course, that it is being provoked by
some militant spokesmen for ethnic minorities," an editorial stated,
"not by Chamber of Commerce study groups or manpower com-
missions for the Department of Labor."[52] The difficulty, then, is
not so much preserving academic standards as it is preserving the
dollar value of a college degree from an upsurgent black underclass.

For some, this racial prospect was alarming. For what the doctrine of open admissions proposed would be to admit this urban
black underclass more readily into the academic groves without the
previous admissions screening that a white, poor and lower middle
class was forced to hurdle. To the struggling bright, white student
who experienced strenuous financial difficulty to obtain a college
degree, a feat that was rightfully regarded as a triumph, open admissions became a threat to his highly valued college credential.
What was more irritating, the underclass demanding *in* was black.
"Can the University Survive the Black Challenge?" *Saturday Review* anxiously asked. For as Education Editor James Cass interpreted it, the "black demands strike more basically at the traditional
concept and function of the university."[53] Although concerned that
open admissions *might* mean the destruction of the urban university,
Saturday Review was plainly more worried over black separatism:
that "some blacks on campus are true revolutionaries and violently
hostile to all things white."[54]

Others such as Irving Kristol and Paul Weaver, editors of the
liberal magazine *The Public Interest*, were perhaps responding more
to the racial overtones than to educational issues. Their fears were
symptomatic of their class—an urban, white, middle-class constituency whose liberalism consisted mainly of an extension of security
benefits to protect *their* interests. The city colleges, they maintained,
had served their (white) immigrant clients well. Now, however,
"black militants are demanding that many more (and, . . . eventually, all) black students who are graduated from high school be admitted automatically to the city colleges, regardless of grades, or
aptitudes, or whatever."[55] The end product, they claimed, would be

the equivalent of "four year community colleges, with all the academic distinction being remorselessly extinguished."[56] These writers feared most the social upheaval entailed when a black, urban poor competes with a now-entrenched middle class.

In 1847, when City College, the first unit of the City University of New York, was established, its stated goal was:

> To bring the advantages of the best education that any school in our country within the reach of all the children in the city whose genius, capacity and desire of attainments are such as to render it reasonably certain that they may be made, and by such means would become, eminently useful to society.[57]

CUNY's goal had been broadened to include students not previously considered "college material." In its initial reactive period, the city entered the field of two-year community colleges and educational skill centers; in 1964, the university's College Discovery Program and Demonstration Guidance Project was begun. That was the first major step towards granting admission to students who were considered inadequately prepared for academic rigors of a four-year college. Other programs have been implemented since then—College Bound, SEEK, 100 Scholars Program. However, it was not until February 28, 1966 that the Board of Higher Education of the City of New York decided to offer the "benefits of post-high school education to all residents of New York City who are *able* and eager to avail themselves of these benefits"—the policy of open admissions—establishing 1975 as the target date.

As a result of the strike at City College, the board adopted a plan that made the following general provisions:

1. It shall offer admission to some University program to all high school graduates of the City.
2. It shall provide for remedial and other supportive services for all students requiring them.
3. It shall maintain and enhance the standards of academic excellence of the colleges of the university.
4. It shall result in the ethnic integration of the colleges.
5. It shall provide mobility for students between various programs and units of the University.

6. It shall assure that students who have been admitted to specific community or senior colleges in the past shall still be so admitted.[58]

Moreover, the board intended to provide for remedial programs to help the new students:

1. The establishment of adequate pre-admissions counseling programs providing students with as much information before making their choice.
2. There must be greatly increased articulation between the colleges of the University and the high schools of the City, particularly in areas of curriculum and guidance.
3. Each college must establish a program to evaluate the strengths and weaknesses of incoming students.
4. Services such as counseling and tutoring assistance should be provided. Special learning conditions, including smaller class size, should be provided.
5. The University should assume the responsibility for insuring that sufficient financial assistance be made available to guarantee that no individual will have economic need interfere with his opportunity for higher education.[59]

Unfortunately, open admissions at CUNY had not overcome inequality. Because of poor recruitment and failure to provide satisfactory remediation, open admissions had not changed much for the better. Like California, most of the 8,500 new black students admitted in the first year were tracked into community colleges, whereas most of the 24,300 white, and largely Catholic, middle-class freshmen were placed in the senior colleges—that despite the fact that two-thirds of students enrolling in community colleges, according to Board of Higher Education figures, desire a four-year degree; in practice only one-sixth transfer to four-year institutions.[60] More rather than less of the top students applied to CUNY.

Choice of college depended on a high school student's grade averages, thus guaranteeing those with higher averages places in the senior college of their choice. To be considered for admission to a senior college, a student first had to attain a grade average of 85 and be in the top 30 percent of his or her class.

Moreover, the open-admissions plan initially failed to offer strong remedial and recruitment programs. The plan did not establish a coordinated remedial policy directed from the top but left such a policy to the discretion of the individual colleges. According to an unpublished study of open admissions at Queens College by Susan Levine, many guidance counsellors did not encourage black students. At Queens, there was a rise from 8.7 percent black and Puerto Rican students in 1969 to between 9 and 13 percent in 1971-72, approximately 1.5 times less than the average for all senior colleges.[61]

Although CUNY succeeded in admitting substantial numbers of black and Puerto Rican students, *compared* to their percentages graduating from city high schools, the two-tiered tracking system of senior and community colleges effectively made for segregated and second-class education. Moreover, students from lower income families were more likely to attend community colleges. Nearly a quarter of the CUNY undergraduates were from families at a poverty level of some $5,000 or less per year in the first year of open admissions.[62]

A major study of open admissions conducted by students concluded that "no American institution of higher education currently operates under a real open admissions policy."[63] That study recommended an open-admissions program that would honor a right to a free higher education that would permit students to "choose which school they wish to attend at no cost."[64] The study especially advocated "the elimination of educational tracks." The student study emerged from what the authors felt was a "deep discontent with the way institutions of higher education are serving students and potential students," and the concomitant "frustration in continually hearing the issues of open admissions misstated, misunderstood and compromised."[65]

Other interpreters of the CUNY experience also agreed that open admissions had failed, but from a different perspective. Opponents of open admissions complained that "education is being ended in America by Tocqueville's 'tyranny of the majority.' "[66] British-born and Oxford-educated Geoffrey Wagner, a City College professor of English, assailed open admissions at CUNY as "so diluting its degree that the place has turned into little more than a diploma mill."[67] Open admissions, Wagner claimed, had, in a few years, made his "task one that could be performed by a janitor." The student open-admissions quality was not only inferior, he maintained, but the demand for relevance had bastardized the curriculum. By a curious inversion of logic and common sense, Wagner assessed the open-admissions experience as one where now "to be Black and poor is the privileged position."[68]

What was expected of open admissions did not come to pass. It was not the full egalitarian program one hoped it would be. Neither did it devalue the university and cause a mass exodus from the urban public universities to the urban private universities as such Cassandras as New York University's James Hester gloomily predicted. In fact, the reverse happened: prospective middle-class students left the urban private universities to attend CUNY. St. John's University reported a 30 percent drop in enrollment the first year of open admissions; the Brooklyn Center of Long Island University revealed that freshman enrollments were down 40 percent for the first two years of open enrollment; and Hester's New York University was so badly affected in enrollment that the university, caught in a financial squeeze, had to go so far as to sell its uptown undergraduate campus to the state university.[69]

Nevertheless, the open-admissions policy of CUNY was short-lived. The financial crisis of New York City in 1975-76 severely affected open admissions at the city university, but not before the experiment had proved not as academically a disaster as its critics had maintained. The graduation and retention rate of the first 1970 open-admissions class was somewhat of an "incomplete success" in the words of one supporter of open admissions.[70] In the senior colleges, 21.4 percent graduated and 35 percent were still enrolled; in the community colleges, 23.1 percent graduated, 2.8 percent went on to a four-year college and 22.2 percent were still enrolled.[71] The large number still enrolled merely indicated the fact that many city students were required to work at least part-time; at Queens College, for example, it was estimated in a survey that as many as 57 percent of the student body held some kind of job. These figures compare favorably nationally with other institutions such as Fairleigh Dickinson, for example, the ninth largest private university, which has a 70 percent attrition rate.[72]

Unfortunately, the policy of free tuition was also victim of the city's financial crisis. City University had stood out, as President Gerald Ford remarked, as the last institution of free tuition in the country (Governor Ronald Reagan had ended the free tuition policy in California in 1970). Public opinion, both in the city and outside, shifted considerably concerning a free urban university. A critical consensus felt that the city had been profligate in its spending and could not afford to maintain a free university system, which, parenthetically, paid the highest faculty salaries in the nation. CUNY was viewed as a luxury in a city that required a federal bailout through loans to avoid bankruptcy. Political leaders of both parties, including President Ford, New York State Governor Carey, and New York City Mayor Beame (himself a product of CUNY and free tuition), led an imperceptible number of foes to free tuition. By spring 1976, the state legislature terminated free tuition at CUNY and instituted a tuition policy similar to the state university with lower classmen paying $750 a year and upper classmen paying $900 a year.

There was little organized resistance from either students, parents, or political and civic leaders. Student organizations, for example, reserved space for some 5,000 picketers outside the Democratic convention in Madison Square Garden in July 1976, only to have less than a dozen students show up to dramatize the fight to save free tuition. One reason for this apathy was that most CUNY students could now qualify for tuition assistance from the state's Tuition Assistance Plan. Those who had to pay most were in the low, middle-income range from $11,000 to $20,000. Still, the State Board of Regents considered extending tuition assistance to students whose families made less than $14,000 (the national average), which accounted for nearly nine out of every ten CUNY students.[73] Despite tuition assistance, however, the CUNY enrollment fell by 17 percent in the first year of tuition.

As for open admissions, its prospects were dim as the program was redesigned. Students for the senior colleges had to obtain an 80 percent high school average or be in the top third of their class. One CUNY sociologist who studies open admissions, David E. Lavin, estimated that the new admissions policy would eliminate 72 percent of black, 65 percent of Puerto Rican, and 20 percent of white prospective students from the CUNY system.[74]

In the end, however, the record of City University indicated that a policy of free tuition and open admissions had attracted many of the urban poor. By the twentieth century, many poor students, especially Jewish students, benefited from free education. The open-admissions policy of the seventies also recruited substantial low-income students. By 1977, some 82 percent were from families with less than $12,000 income, and a majority came from low-income families.[75] A policy of free tuition and open admissions proved to have significantly recruited the urban poor.

NOTES

1. David F. Allmendinger, Jr., *Paupers and Scholars* (New York: St. Martins Press, 1975), p. 59.

2. Michael Young, *The Rise of the Meritocracy* (Middlesex, Eng.: Penguin, 1961), p. 94.

3. Daniel Bell, *The Coming of Post-Industrial Society* (New York: Basic Books, 1973), p. 411.

4. Ibid., p. 426.

5. Ibid.

6. Samuel Bowles and Herbert Gintis, *Schooling in Capitalist America* (New York: Basic Books, 1976), p. 105.

7. Michael Useem and S. M. Miller, "The Upper Class in Higher Education," *Social Policy*, January-February 1977, p. 30.

8. Edward Danforth Eddy, Jr., *Colleges for Our Land and Time: The Land-Grant Idea in American Education* (New York: Harper & Brothers, 1957), p. 85.

9. Keith W. Olson, *The G.I. Bill, the Veterans, and the Colleges* (Lexington, Ky.: The University Press of Kentucky, 1974), p. 44.

10. Ibid., p. 35.

11. Ibid., p. 51.

12. Bell, *The Coming of Post-Industrial Society*, p. 410.

13. Jerome Karabel, "Perspectives on Open Admissions," *Educational Record* 53, no. 1 (Winter 1972): 42.

14. Ibid., pp. 42-43.

15. Randall Collins, "Some Comparative Principles of Educational Stratification," *Harvard Educational Review* 47, no. 1 (February 1977): 21.

16. Frederic Rudolph, *The American College and University* (New York: Knopf, 1962), p. 216.

17. Parke Kolbe, *Urban Influences in Higher Education in England and the United States* (New York: Macmillian, 1928), p. 196.

18. Allmendinger, *Paupers and Scholars*, p. 65.

19. Ibid., p. 18.

20. S. Willis Rudy, *The College of the City of New York: A History 1847-1947* (New York: The City College Press, 1949), pp. 68-69.

21. Rudolph, *The American College and University*, p. 219.

22. Ibid., p. 278.

23. Ibid., p. 216.

24. Ibid., p. 254.

25. Eddy, *Colleges for Our Land*, p. 116.

26. Rudolph, *The American College and University*, p. 281.

27. Colin Greer, *The Great School Legend* (New York: Basic Books, 1972), p. 121.

28. Ora E. Reynolds, *The Social and Economic Status of College Students* (New York: Teachers College Press, 1927), pp. 13-14.

29. Ibid., p. 23.

30. Bowles and Gintis, *Schooling in Capitalist America*, p. 8.

31. National Center for Educational Statistics, *The Condition of Education* (Washington: U.S. Government Printing Office, 1976), p. 89.

32. Torsten Husen, "The Equality-Meritocracy Dilemma in Education," in *Education, Inequality, and National Policy*, Nelson F. Ashline et al., eds. (Lexington, Mass.: Lexington Books, D. C. Heath, 1976), p. 47.

33. Warren Willingham, *Free-access Higher Education* (Princeton: College Entrance Examination Board, 1970), p. 212.

34. Urban Research Corporation, *Student Protests 1969* (Chicago: 1970), p. 5.

35. Timothy S. Healy, "Will Everyman Destroy the University?" *Saturday Review*, December 20, 1969, p. 55.

36. Michael S. Schudson, "Organizing the 'Meritocracy': A History of the College Entrance Examination Board," *Harvard Educational Review* 42, no. 1 (February 1972): 35.

37. Ibid., p. 67.

38. Robert Williams, "What We Are Learning from Current Programs for Disadvantaged Students," *Journal of Higher Education* XL, no. 4 (April 1969): 276.

39. A. J. Jaffe and Walter Adams, "Open Admissions and Academic Quality," *Change*, March-April 1971, p. 11.

40. Ibid.

41. Ibid.

42. Nadine Brozan, "Life on a Treadmill: Financing College for

Several Children," *New York Times,* October 21, 1976, p. 34.

43. Carnegie Council on Policy Studies in Higher Education, *Low or No Tuition* (San Francisco: Jossey-Bass, 1975), p. 25.

44. *Newsweek,* June 9, 1969, p. 91.

45. Albert Bowker, *Queens College Report,* Fall 1969, p. 5.

46. David Rosen, Seth Brunner, and Steve Fowler, *Open Admissions: The Promise & The Lie of Open Access to American Higher Education* (Lincoln, Neb.: University of Nebraska Press, 1973), p. 51.

47. *New York Times,* May 26, 1969, p. 1.

48. Michael Harrington, "College Entrance," *Long Island Press,* June 1, 1969, p. 18.

49. Urban Research Corporation, *Student Protests 1969,* p. 11.

50. Ibid.

51. Spiro Agnew, "Toward a 'Middle Way' in College Admissions," *Educational Record,* Spring 1970, pp. 107-10.

52. *Saturday Review,* June 21, 1969, p. 64.

53. James Cass, "Can the University Survive the Black Challenge," *Saturday Review,* June 21, 1969, p. 68.

54. Ibid., p. 83.

55. Irving Kristol and Paul Weaver, "Who Knows New York? Notes on a Mixed-up City," *The Public Interest,* no. 16 (Summer 1969): 45.

56. Ibid.

57. Susan Levine, "Open Admissions at Queens College," New York: 1971, p. 3.

58. Ibid., p. 5.

59. Ibid., p. 6.

60. Ibid., p. 8.

61. Ibid., p. 10.

62. Rosen, Brunner, and Fowler, *Open Admissions,* p. 161.

63. Ibid., p. 1.

64. Ibid.

65. Ibid., p. 7.

66. Geoffrey Wagner, *The End of Education* (New York: A.S. Barnes, 1976), p. 13.

67. Ibid., p. 237.

68. Ibid., p. 89.

69. Levine, "Open Admissions," p. 20.

70. Michael Harrington, "Keep Open Admissions Open," *New York Times Magazine,* November 2, 1975, p. 4.

71. Ibid.

72. Conversation with David Watson, director of institutional research, Fairleigh Dickinson University, October 22, 1976.

73. *New York Times*, October 29, 1976, p. B. 18.

74. Larry Van Dyne, "The Free-Tuition Fight Is Lost," *Chronicle of Higher Education*, September 20, 1976, p. 5.

75. Interview with Jack Sullivan, director of university relations, City University, May 24, 1977 (Phone).

CHAPTER 3

The urban university as neighbor

There has been a historic tradition that has slowed the pace of the urban university. This anti-urban animus has dictated campus expansion relations with surrounding poor communities. Ours has been basically an anti-city temper. Ingrained in the American psyche has been an affinity for the ideal of land. The richness and variety of America's space has deeply permeated our angle of vision. America's novelists and poets, speaking our innermost thoughts, connoted a rich, romantic tradition against the city. Great romanticists and transcendentalists such as Jefferson, Emerson, Thoreau, Hawthorne, Poe, Melville, Twain, Henry Adams, Dreiser, Frank Lloyd Wright, Hemingway, and Kerouac have envisioned the city as evil incarnate. The city is where innocence ends and corruption begins. This anti-city temper emanates, to a great extent, from a harsh Calvinism that pictures the city not as a breeding place of culture but as a fount of crime and evil. One's Christian duty is to combat this evil. This Calvinistic view permeated the romantic vision.

By contrast, the American frontier, as Frederick Jackson Turner argued, best defined the American character. The image of the frontiersman, misanthrophically quitting the evils of city life, recurs throughout American mythology: Natty Bumppo thrives in the forest; Ishmael at sea; Huckleberry Finn on the Mississippi; Jake Barnes in the mountains; and Sal Paradise on the road. This is the stuff of the archetypal American culture hero: the pilgrim forever in progress, the moral cowboy in the eternal American western.

To Europeans, the city was far from being a dark place. For Voltaire, London was the light of the enlightenment where "Men

44

speak their thoughts and work can win its place. In London, who has talent, he is great."[1] Far from being hell, the city was the fount of virtue, grace, and civilization. Even social reformers such as Marx and Engels saw the potentialities of the city man. "Only the proletariat," Engels wrote, "herded in big cities is in a position to accomplish the great social transformation which will put an end to all class exploitation and all class rule."[2]

This anti-urban bias of American intellectuals has been partly traced to an agrarian tradition developed early in America. American Colonial intellectuals lived not in the European walled city, but on small estates and farms possessing small land holdings. Today, a majority of American intellectuals are home owners, rather than apartment dwellers, with their own backyards. The larger number of European intellectuals, on the other hand, live in apartments. A majority of the faculty at New York's Columbia University, for example, live not in the city but in the surrounding suburbs.

The consequence of this aversion to the city was the pastoral college. The pastoral college has long clouded the higher education landscape. The city was not considered conducive to the rarefied atmosphere of learning. "Who can study in Boston streets," John Adams queried. For Adams, the humanity of the colonial city concocted a cacophony that filled his ears with "the rattle-gabble of them all" so he could not "think long enough in the street upon any one thing, to start and pursue a thought."[3]

This view, suspecting the darker strains of human nature, blending with an affinity for America's gigantic space, colored the viewpoint of American educators. They ignored the European medieval tradition of establishing universities in the town. Cities were a way of life since the Middle Ages, and most European universities were urban. They were situated in the great European cities for the same reasons they are today: the city is civilization; it attracts, holds, and preserves the finance and the leisure only wealth can bring, which is necessary for culture. The city complements great universities as great universities complement the city.

Nevertheless, Americans chose to emulate the English suburban tradition of countryside colleges. These colleges proclaimed the romantic virtues of the country, of the bucolic, small New England

college. This myth is anti-city, anti-people, and anti-poor. According to the standard version of this myth, college America is a lei-
surely Socratic stroll in a small town, nestled in ivy and surrounded
by elms, and isolated from the citizens.

In the eighteenth and nineteenth centuries, some state governments, when granting their charters, went so far as to forbid new
universities from locating in cities.[4] As late as 1878, a popular collegiate guide deplored the university in the city: "If Yale were located at Williamstown, Harvard at Hanover, Columbia at Ithaca,
the moral character of their students would be elevated in as great
a degree as the natural scenery of their localities would be increased
in beauty."[5]

In addition to the distrust of cities by the Puritans, the development of the land-grant college in the mid-nineteenth century fur-
thered the pastoral myth. The land-grant state colleges were located
far from large cities in isolated areas. That was partly because of
the need for space for the study of agriculture, for which the land-
grant colleges were created. As a result, a larger economic reality
bolstered the pastoral collegiate myth, since young America had
been basically an agrarian nation. Only the Catholic colleges in the
nineteenth century were situated in the cities to serve their urban,
ethnic clientele better. Today, however, these Catholic, urban universities find their constituencies have begun the trek to the suburbs.

In the past generation, urban educators and planners have displayed an aversion to the city and its ghettoes. One educator,
Jacques Barzun, while provost of Columbia University, branded
the community as "uninviting, abnormal, sinister, dangerous . . . the
relationship of students and faculty to the community requires
the perpetual *qui vive* of a paratrooper in enemy country."[6] The
imperative was to relocate the poor. For city planner Roger Starr,
Columbia was performing a social service by purchasing "buildings for rehabilitation . . . to get rid of 'undesirables' . . . goals—
less crime, less slumminess—which respectable neighbors trea-
sure. . . ."[7]

The university president was presented with a problem: how to
accommodate the ever-growing housing needs of a burgeoning
campus as well as create a more humane environment for the urban
university. In the last few years, the problem has become exacer-

bated by the dramatic rise of violent crime in the urban slums. Students and faculty have in many instances become victims of violence.

It was inevitable that there should be, in time, confrontations between the urban university and the community in which it was situated. As the cities began to deteriorate in the last generation, with more poor occupying the central core and the middle class exodusing to the outlying suburbs, the relationship between urban university and urban community became strained.

The most comprehensive analysis of these town-gown relations, among 102 urban universities surveyed during a twenty-year period between 1952 and 1972, found that nearly 80 percent reported some "level of tension with neighbors."[8] Of that percentage, one-fifth of the urban universities revealed "frequent or severe" relations with their neighbors. Understandably, the larger the urban university and the larger the city, the more exacerbated the relations. The study observed that "of those universities with an enrollment over 25,000 and located in cities larger than 1,700,000 . . . 80% reported frequent or severe tensions."[9] It is clear that the urban university has experienced troubling relations with its city neighbors in recent times.

The nature of the urban university's trouble has varied. In one instance, it has involved the fruits of knowledge. The city of Cambridge expressed alarm over Harvard University experiments scheduled with new and unknown forms of life with deoxyribonucleic acid (DNA). These experiments in genetic research have frightened the townspeople who were wary that Harvard scientists might create, in Mayor Alfred Velucci's phrase, a "Frankenstein germ" that might infect the townspeople.[10] However, most of the disputes with the urban universities have concerned the expansion into the neighboring community.

These confrontations were subtle and sophisticated, political land struggles afflicting, in most cases, those least able to afford affliction —the poor in the surrounding communities. They were relocated from their homes to join a restless army of urban refugees in search of new homes and new roots, merely to preserve the myth of the agrarian American campus.

Yet, only within the past generation has the American academic community been taken to task for its agrarian myth. The answer of the American urban university to the demands of growth and expansion has been to push the stale and irrelevant myth of the pastoral college. The poor are uprooted, their buildings razed, and a new bucolic piece of campus annexed to the pastoral urban university. It is this relation of gown to town that has brought upon American universities their severest criticisms and some of their most potentially explosive crises. The sad fact has been that the urban university is distrusted in the cities by its encircling poor.

The American urban university administrator had been blind to the most elementary principles. From his agrarian unconscious, he had seen only one solution to the urban university's growth problems: expand. As the urban universities attracted more students, developed greater research capabilities, and hired more staff, the urban university administrator sought more land to house his temple of scholarship. That view meant a bulldozing approach that has wholly disregarded the natural constituents of the city.

There is the European example before us. Urban universities have been created using the existing natural habitats of the city, without the need to tear down and reconstruct the environs. The European university employs the natural beauties of the city, so the urban university is but a collection of varied buildings blending into the landscape. It is a university that highlights the best in urban life and gives a pulse to the varied atmosphere of a city. Go to any American city and visit the landlocked pastoral island. Then visit Heidelberg and capture the charm and beauty of an integrated landscape of the urban university. That expanse of green testifies to the American's distrust of the city.

It is, of course, more complicated than just a set of assumptions Americans have failed to question rigorously. The urban university is far from the monastic ideal some administrators may have considered. Rather, the American urban university is a wealthy businessman in the affairs of the city. Boston's colleges are the largest business in the city—$1.3 billion; the University of Pittsburgh is the second largest employer in that city; Columbia is one of the richest land owners in New York City.[11] These urban universities pay in the millions for wages and real estate taxes to the cities. They also attract subsidiary industries dependent on university research. In short, the urban university is a city power to reckon with.

The fact of the urban university's power is all the more reason that it should pursue enlightened urban policies. Certainly, the urban poor are aware and in fear of this economic giant. Columbia University, for example, has used its economic strength to no small advantage. Columbia has assets of nearly $.5 billion and an annual payroll of some $100 million. Since 1957 Columbia bought $12 million of buildings on the Heights with this effect: the university acquired some 150 buildings, displaced some 7,500 individuals, and reduced apartments 12 percent and single-room units 70 percent.[12] With some irony, Columbia students could chant the ditty— "Who owns New York? C-O-L-U-M-B-I-A." This economic clout brings a clear message: The urban poor share a common fear of the urban university. The fear of being trampled by the wealth of the urban university exists side by side with the symbol of the university as a gateway to economic security. The poor have long been drummed on the tune that education means jobs. The university is society's certification tool, the Calvinistic instrument, that endows one as being among the socioeconomic elect of this country. It has often placed itself in an adversary position to the poor.

The urban university's conflict has had many unpleasant effects. One has been violent: demonstrations. But there have been less noticeable ones. The urban university has lost its credibility in the ghetto. Increasingly, the life-styles of the poor are becoming difficult to study. Sociologists, political scientists, and anthropologists are turned off and turned away by the inhabitants of city slums. They are served notice that they are not wanted. The urban university has so antagonized its city neighbors that it has lost its ability to perform its functions in one vital area of modern and city life: the study of the poor. It is the legacy of the agrarian and Calvinistic myth.

The urban university finds itself checkmated by the city. Many communities have successfully thwarted efforts of urban universities to expand. Temple University and the University of Pennsylvania have been pressured by community opposition to delay construction plans for more facilities. Tufts' plans to locate a medical center in a cramped Chinese ghetto in Boston—2,000 people in an eight-square-block area—was stalled by young Chinese activists. What was once considered a mild public relations problem on the part of university officials now looms as crisis.

More important, the urban university's land policies have become bad politics. Boston's Mayor Kevin White, for example, was responsive in the 1970 election year to Bostonians' protest against Boston College expansion. The growing resentment of Boston's public to the urban-removal policies of its educational institutions spread to middle-class whites. Boston College officials wisely sidestepped the lure to build in ghettoes for fear of expected heated opposition. Instead, they sought to purchase luxury apartment houses, only to be met by equally strong opposition. Since the middle-class inhabitants were more politically organized than the poor, they were able to have the mayor change zoning regulations to halt the proposed expansion.[13]

The opposition to university expansion crosses class lines. The University of Pittsburgh's expansion plans were opposed by the black poor, a white middle class and a wealthy group of home owners. In 1964, 3,000 middle-class home owners organized against the university's efforts to build in a business and residential area.[14] This was followed some years later by a successful black protest to the university's possible expansion in the city's largest black ghetto.

Part of the problem has been that a national policy for urban universities had encouraged them to pursue their agrarian myth. In 1959, Congress passed Section 112 of the National Housing Act, which was hailed as a veritable urban Homestead Act by virtually every urban university administrator in the nation. Section 112 made life optimistic to the university president anxious about expanding in the slums. Under the terms of that provision, universities would receive three dollars of federal urban-renewal assistance for every dollar spent on "acquisition of land, buildings or structures within, adjacent to or in the immediate vicinity of, an urban renewal project, for demolition . . . for relocation of occupants and for rehabilitation of buildings" used for educational purposes.[15] The urban university was given carte blanche to clean up its slums, solve its land problem, and make a nice profit in the bargain. According to the complicated mechanics of Section 112, the city government would receive federal urban-renewal aid and in turn would credit urban universities to purchase land from the city earmarked for urban renewal at one-fifth of its cost on the open market. In six years, Section 112 resulted in 77 urban university-renewal projects already begun and nearly 200 about to be started.[16]

Section 112 constituted a strong national policy. That policy, ironically enough, had been praised as a "*rapproachement* between universities and cities." Cornell Professor K. C. Parsons, had applauded Section 112 as the beginning of a "truce in the war between the universities and cities."[17] Soon after J. Martin Klotscke, in *The Urban University and the Future of Our Cities*, could applaud Section 112 as helping to solve Columbia's land problems as well as those of similarly situated urban universities. Reinforcing these hopes were the sentiments of urban-renewal bureaucrats that Section 112, would provide the leadership for such noble experiments as Columbia's and the University of Chicago's slum-clearance projects.

In a trenchant analysis of the workings of Section 112, William Deane Smith of the Center for Urban Studies at Detroit's Wayne State University minced no words concerning the poisoning of the community atmosphere. "Wayne State University," Smith posed in a policy proposal, "has in the past few years acquired nearly one hundred acres of land via urban renewal. In doing so, the University has also acquired a reputation of being the 'enemy' of the local resident."[18] Smith pointed up the contradiction implicit in the urban universities' scholarly service function to urban students vis-à-vis their displacement land policies:

It is generally acknowledged, especially by educators, that the very services being proposed for Central Detroit are the same ones needed for our "disadvantaged" population to assure their children of becoming "advantaged." To what end, then, would the removal of this population from the area where these services will be available?[19]

The study concluded that no citywide comprehensive planning had been devised. Rather, there was but a cacophony of self-interest. The university's 33,000 students and 4,000 faculty and staff formed no visible community but consisted of a "migratory population which uses the facilities of the University but does not contribute to the life of the community."[20] In the short run, university "redevelopment doctrines" would only increase friction with neighboring communities. In the long run, the prospects were bleak since there existed no public programs "with real promise of improving the quality of life for those who now occupy the area . . . rather such programs have been and are now being provided for those who will replace the present residents."[21]

Smith's candid analysis was all the more forceful since his own university was scrutinized. He was not passionately flailing away at some other's sins; rather, he performed the more difficult task of excoriating his own employer. All the more significant then were his suggestions for what the university should do. Conceptually, Smith wrote that the universities "must be viewed as the primary sources of pressure for change" rather than merely search out their self-interest.[22]

The classic example of bad community relations has been Columbia. The 1968 Columbia student strike was in part caused by the university's callous land dealings. What university officials and bureaucrats were loudly proclaiming as the salvation of Morningside Heights was grinding slowly towards a confrontation with national implications. Many factors led to the Columbia uprising. There was the issue of defense research for the warfare state. There was the realization that Columbia was quietly slipping into a second-rank institution: faculty salaries had dropped from fifth to seventeenth place; since 1965, faculty were leaving because, according to the Cox Commission Report, of being "openly upset over the institutional conditions under which they had to work";[23] by mid-1966, Columbia had shown a decline in the quality of its graduate programs in the last decade, according to the American Council on Education, so it dropped from among the first three to as low as tenth place; the Ford Foundation in 1967 overlooked Columbia in a major grant to ten leading universities in devising innovative doctoral programs.

This academic deterioration established the background for the events that were to follow. Yet, of equal import was the university's hostility to the urban environment. Columbia administrators regarded its urban communities in Barzun's revealing phrase as being in the way—"a paratrooper in enemy country"—and this attitude filtered down to faculty. For all the pious proclamations of an urban community of scholars, fully 50 percent of Columbia's staff from assistant professor up live outside of Manhattan and over 40 percent live outside New York City.[24] Those figures cannot be interpreted primarily as a lack of suitable living quarters for faculty. In the borough of Queens, for example, only one-fifth of Queens College faculty and staff live in nearby Nassau County; most reside in the suburbanized city borough. College faculties merely follow the larger suburban trends. They are not exceptional in this matter. A great proportion of city schoolteachers, firemen, and policemen live in the suburbs rather than in the city.

This residential faculty pattern is anti-urban. Moreover, Columbia had not instituted any major urban-studies programs. As of the 1968 disturbances, only one New York college—Hunter—offered urban studies. Only if one considers the generally slow pace of urbanization in American higher education can this development be considered progress. But, confronted with the reality of urban growth after World War II, this small collegiate concern in urban issues constitutes a severe cultural lag. In the early 1930s only eleven institutions in nine cities could be characterized as municipal (city-run) universities; and only New York City could be considered a major city with a municipal university system. Columbia, then, was not singular in its neglect of its urban environment.

Columbia's proposed gymnasium symbolized the urban land question. Of itself, the gym was of slight importance. Columbia had intended to build a gym adjacent to its Morningside Heights campus. The gym was to be used both by students and the Harlem community below. The gym, however, became a symbol of university callousness to its black poor neighbors in much the same fashion as the windowless public school IS 201 affronted the black community a few years previous. The gym would have two separate entrances, one for students and one for Harlem residents; Columbia was to receive 87.5 percent of the space and the community 12.5 percent.

What was particularly noxious to the black community was that the land for the gym was public park land. When considered with the long list of Columbia land expansions with little thought of the black community, the Columbia gym was a final insult. An ad hoc committee against the gym had been formed early, representing the Harlem political establishment. Indeed, so great was the opposition that John Lindsay, running for mayor in 1965, had issued a white paper condemning the gym because the Harlem community should determine largely for itself how best to use its park lands and because park property should not be allowed to go to private use. Meetings between the committee and Columbia were held in 1966-67, with the university taking a hard line that there could not be any mutual sharing of the gym. Columbia, however, would be gracious enough to add a swimming pool for the community. A more militant community group, the West Side Harlem Morningside Park Committee, was formed for stronger action. This group staged rallies and demonstrations including a construction blockade on February 19, 1968 that resulted in six students and six community residents arrested, an act that was a prelude to the spring strike.

The gym was an affront to the black community. To be built on a hill, from community park land, the upper level was to accommodate Columbia students and the lower level, black residents. The physical juxtaposition of the gym atop a hill campus overlooking Harlem was not lost on blacks who had been weaned on blues and spirituals accepting the difference of "living in the lowlands." Columbia's Students for a Democratic Society focused on the gym among its many complaints against the university.

For Columbia President Grayson Kirk there was no problem. Columbia was prepared to invest nearly $11 million in an athletic field and gym and had secured the official permit from the Parks Department for the land. The troublemakers were some citizens who had no interest in the gymnasium project per se but who were opposed to the physical expansion of the university on the Heights, and who seized upon the project as a means of causing trouble generally for Columbia. Maintaining the attitude of a paratrooper in enemy land, Kirk reasoned that Harlem youngsters would be the eventual losers should the gym not be built at the Columbia location. A gym would definitely be built somewhere in the city, he stated, and black youngsters could be without a recreational facility.

There was a much more important principle at stake, however—

one that eluded President Kirk. The university had failed to take the community into consultation on its plans. That was the main issue in the Columbia gym. As such, Columbia thus inadvertantly gave poor communities a powerful argument for community control of institutions, public or "private," that affect the public interest. The Cox Commission plainly scored the university on this point: "Whether the gymnasium was good or bad for Harlem, public property was being used for private purposes and the new spokesman for the increasingly self-conscious black community of the mid-1960's has no share in the planning or decisions."[25]

The intransigence of Columbia's administrators on the gym during the disturbances was difficult to fathom. The Ad Hoc Faculty Group's (AHFG's) "bitter-pill" settlement plan, which gave the community veto power over the construction of the gym, was particularly rejected out of hand by President Kirk on that point. Whatever the misconception a vested interest such as the AHFG had in presenting a compromise plan not especially satisfying to both parties—a "bitter pill" as the Columbia Daily Spectator staff characterized it—it was by all means the most sensible solution offered in those crisis days. Nevertheless, at no point did the university administrators intend to change their course of action regarding the gym. Moreover, the full faculty vote, disregarding the high aims of the ad hoc group, endorsed a resolution strengthening the administration's position. One small consolation was that the police refrained from brutality in evicting the black students from Hamilton Hall; however, the police did terrorize the white radical students. The aftermath was as bloody. A president of a university resigned in failure; many of its best faculty—conservative, liberal, and radical—opted out of the university as did students; and the mark of a second-rate institution was branded on a once leading Ivy-League institution. No one won. There was some talk of student participation on the restructuring of the university but there were little imaginative results. A commission to investigate the disturbances headed by Archibald Cox produced a small classic example of clear-headed thinking and integral values among the plethora of bias written on Columbia. The gym was stopped.

But Columbia did not learn much from its lesson in community relations. The Ford Foundation donated some $10 million for an urban center to improve the university's credit with its black neighborhoods. The center was headed by a prestigious black, Franklin Williams, a former Democratic ambassador to Ghana, who presided over a rich subcontracting operation that accomplished little. Three professorial chairs were underwritten from the first $5 million. None of the money was earmarked for projects that would build up community housing. None of the Ford monies was reinvested in the Harlem communities. After much rhetoric, the center produced its answer to the crisis of the urban university. A long study, *The Human Uses of the University*, mainly urged the creation of a joint Urban and Black Studies curriculum that appeared adequate. The report was silent on the university's land policies. Instead, it recommended an Ethnic and Urban Research Information and Community Center. This agency was to establish a joint community-university committee to determine common programs.[26] By 1973, the Urban Center was quietly abolished.

What could not happen at Harvard did. Like Columbia, Harvard was the focus of a campus revolt in the same spring of 1968 largely over the issue of war and the draft. The immediate issue was that of banning the ROTC. However, students seized on the urban university's expansion policies to buttress their case against the school. But, unlike Columbia, Harvard's expansion did not loom as a significant cause of the Harvard strike. It was an afterthought.

Nevertheless, it was symbolic that America's best and most honored university should also follow narrow policies. The land problem was "discovered" early in the year by the local poverty agency. The Cambridge Economic Opportunity Committee had surveyed housing facilities for the elderly. They were shocked to learn that 57 of those surveyed paid more than half of their income for rent and heat; a reasonable rule of thumb for rentals is an average of one-fourth of one's income. The poverty agency then organized some 800 residents into a pressure group called the Cambridge Housing Convention (CHC), which resolved to seek the help of the city government, the universities, and redevelopment groups in alleviating the low-income housing shortage. It particularly criticized Harvard and Massachusetts Institute of Technology (MIT).

A series of meetings with CHC, Harvard, and MIT administrators proved futile.

Instead, the universities responded in characteristic fashion with yet another study—a preliminary report for the two universities by Professor James Q. Wilson—that delineated the role of the university and the city. The Wilson report constituted a mild rebuke of the university's land policies. Wilson sought the best of both worlds, the mixing of housing for the poor and the middle class, creating a truly integrated community. The report failed to lay blame on the university, which owned nearly 300 non-university housing units in Cambridge. It did, however, urge Harvard and MIT to work with community groups "in helping Cambridge develop a larger program for publicly assisted housing."[27] The report merely advised the universities to help in relocation of the poor in expansion and at the same time "seek out appropriate sites within Cambridge on which housing for faculty and students may be built." Wilson sought to please all factions: *It is vital that the supply of low-income housing (especially for the elderly) and of moderate cost housing (for both faculty and community residents) be increased.*[28]

The Wilson Report was ignored. The Harvard administration took only one recommendation out of context—appointing a new presidential assistant for "local relations" as an advisory rather than a general planner, as Wilson advocated. The faculty of Arts and Sciences refused to consider the report. There was little student interest. After canvassing the campus from January to April attempting "to sell them on the idea that there *was* a problem," Wilson was able to secure only the Divinity School's endorsement. At no time were there more than two dozen people at a meeting on the report, none of whom asked more than routine questions or showed more than slight interest. Wilson scored university apathy at a general School of Education meeting in late March.

If the university was bored, the Cambridge community was not. An offshoot of the Radical Peace and Freedom party in Cambridge, the Cambridge Rent Control Referendum Campaign, kept things at a boil. They lambasted the Wilson report as "the officially approved whitewash of Harvard's urban policy" and sought a referendum to force "an immediate freeze on all Harvard owned buildings" and a moratorium on Harvard construction.[29] Instead, they advocated that Harvard build low-income housing on its own land for students and the community poor. They reasoned thus:

Harvard, MIT and the other speculators have adopted a self-conscious policy of converting Cambridge to an "upper-middle-class" town because "life will be simpler" for the administrations of the Universities. However, if they succeed, life will be a great deal harder for workers and students, [who will] both be driven out to make way for engineers and other professionals. There is nowhere to go. They will be paying higher rents for worse housing if the low income housing they now occupy is destroyed. Students have a common interest with the people of Cambridge in fighting to stop the rape of our city.[30]

Students for a Democratic Society (SDS) made expansion a campus issue by supporting the referendum. Michael Kazin, an SDS leader and son of the literary critic Alfred Kazin, strongly argued that Harvard establish a low-income housing project for the Cambridge poor, a demand that SDS maintained throughout the strike.

The confrontation lingered through the seventies. A community group disrupted the 1970 Harvard commencement exercises demanding that over 100,000 square feet of vacant property owned by Harvard be made available for low-rent housing. "We are the oppressed people," Mrs. Saundra Graham, the leader of the protestors, announced. "We are tired of Harvard coming into the area and taking our homes."[31] Five years later, senior-class orator Orrin Tilevitz would declare that ". . . Harvard owns an important part of Cambridge, the way the British used to own most of Africa. The reaction of the natives is reportedly the same."[32]

A third major confrontation of the urban university and its community occurred the following year at Berkeley. What was called the "Battle of Berkeley" concerned an unused piece of recently acquired university land that the Berkeley community had transformed into a "people's park" through squatters' rights. The dispute over the park erupted into violence, with the loss of one young man's life.

University regents purchased a lot in 1968 for possible development. Buildings were razed, but the land was little used, except as an informal parking lot. In the spring of 1969, the neighboring community, mixed of poor and student radicals and "street-people," decided to occupy the park for community purposes. A number of projects were conceived including a child-care clinic and a crafts fair. Meanwhile, the park began being used by children, students, and the elderly. At this point, the university, fearing a possible loss of the lot, decided to act. They fenced the people's park and ringed it with county police. Some 3,000 community residents angrily gathered and threw rocks at police, only to receive a fusillade from police that resulted in the death of a twenty-five-year-old, the blinding of another citizen, and the wounding of thirty others. Police operations brought the wrath of some 200 faculty members who protested through a work stoppage, the condemnation of labor and church groups, editorial criticism, and a student referendum in favor of the community. The student referendum was especially significant since 85 percent of the 15,000 voting students wanted the park to remain. Furthermore, the students polled decided to assess themselves $1.50 each to help finance an ethnic studies department at the university. In the end, the university prevailed. People's park was transformed into a fenced parking lot.[33]

The Battle of Berkeley was one in a long list of university-community disagreements. For some time, the university has pursued its Calvinistic purpose to rid the "area not only of sub-standard housing but its human blight."[34] In a sense, the Battle of Berkeley was inevitable, giving the university administrators mind-set.

One of the first confrontations of new urban universities with its slums was in Chicago. Since the early 1950s, the University of Chicago relentlessly bought slum property in Hyde Park-Kenwood and "renewed" it into a middle-class community. The poor were displaced. Initially, the university embarked on its mission after a prolonged crime wave in 1952. The university's efforts involved obtaining favorable state legislation in 1953 in redevelopment. The Chicago group then succeeded in pressing Congress in 1959 to amend the urban renewal laws. Thus, they were responsible for Section 112. The Chicago example was hailed throughout the country as the solution to the university and its problem of slum neighbors. Julian Levi, a key figure in the Chicago story, bally-hooed the Chicago plan to diverse urban institutions such as the University of Pennsylvania, Harvard, MIT, and Columbia.[35]

But the Chicago story had an upbeat note. By the mid-sixties, the Woodlawn Organization (a pioneer, radical, community activist group founded by organizer Saul Alinsky) persuaded Mayor Daley and the University of Chicago to invest in some low-rent housing in the neighborhood. As a result, the Woodlawn Gardens was built from federal and foundation money—a low-cost apartment complex.[36]

One major explanation for the moderation of university policy vis-à-vis low-income communities has been their structure. For the most part, key policy has been established by administrations accountable to lay boards of trustees. These boards often represent the dominant class in society.

One need only examine the trustees of any urban institution to discover a strong force for the status quo. Any private university such as Columbia is governed mainly by pillars of the middle and upper class of Americans, the inheritors of the American way. These men, successful in business and other endeavors, having done well by America, are convinced that the system works. Of twenty-one active trustees (non-emeritus) in 1970 after the disturbances, eighteen were listed in *Who's Who in America*. They represented the top managerial class in the nation, from such conservative fields as the law, finance, and communications. Two were prominent attorneys, one was a judge, and another was the district attorney of Manhattan county. One owned and managed the *New York Times*, the only newspaper national in scope, and one managed a large motion picture company. Another was the chief executive of CBS, one of the nation's leading radio and television networks. Four were financiers with influential banks. Six were business executives of large firms in utilities, telephone, publishing, drugs, and merchandising. One was an architect-businessman. None was a poet, writer, or scholar. None was poor. Only one of the three *not* in *Who's Who* had some background in poverty, a black official of the Bedford Stuyvesant poverty agency, and he was appointed in 1969 after the troubles, presumably as a concession to the black community.[37]

As James Ridgeway observed in *The Closed Corporation*, board membership is a two-way street: business executives not only sit on university boards but university presidents are represented on corporate boards. By Ridgeway's count, no less than eighty-four university officials sat on the boards of major corporations.[38] Similarly, the board members of a private urban university are greatly removed and have little contact with America's underclass. Such board members, like their counterparts in suburban public school boards, have little reason to seek radical university reform. They are satisfied more or less with the basic thrust of higher education, disturbed only by a radical professor or two. They do not have the motivation of the black city poor; the black poor seek to reform public schools to correct the failure of their children. They do not have the motivation of poor citizens in the city who are threatened by the expanding urban university next door.

By the early seventies, groups such as the Carnegie Commission on Higher Education would issue precautions about university expansion in the city. Although acknowledging the problem of obtaining more housing by urban universities, Carnegie advised that urban administrators "limit their need for expansion into scarce urban space by better use of existing space."[39]

Federal housing policy underwent significant change in the seventies. Under Title VII of the Housing and Urban Development Act of 1970, the federal government sought to promote community development projects. Some of these resulted in a few urban universities building low- and moderate-income housing. That policy, however, was not as direct and as bold as Section 112, which furnished monies. Title VII encouraged construction of low-cost housing by universities by offering loan guarantees to private developers. By 1973, categorical grants for urban renewal were ended and replaced by revenue sharing for community development, which some observers felt redirected the flow of federal funds to small towns and suburbs and away from central cities.[40] The Housing and Community Development Act of 1974 took a backward step by eliminating monies for any projects dealing with housing or schools.

In retrospect, the urban university's problems with neighboring communities in expansion were a result of federal urban-renewal policies. Had these policies been more mindful of repercussions, they could have played a beneficial role in creating greater harmony between the university and the city.

NOTES

1. Carl E. Schorske, "The Idea of the City in European Thought: Voltaire to Spengler," in *The Historian and The City*, eds. Oscar Handlin and John Burchard (Cambridge: MIT Press, 1963), p. 97.

2. Ibid., p. 106.

3. Frank Freidel, "Boosters, Intellectuals, and the American City," in *The Historian and the City*, eds. Oscar Handlin and John Burchard (Cambridge: MIT Press, 1963), p. 119.

4. Frederic Rudolph, *The American College and University* (New York: Knopf, 1962), p. 92.

5. Ibid., p. 93.

6. Joanne Grant, *Confrontation on Campus* (New York: Signet, 1969), p. 29.

7. Roger Starr, "The Case of the Columbia Gym," *The Public Interest*, no. 13 (Fall 1968): 105.

8. Robert L. Carroll et al., *University-Community Tension and Urban Campus Form* (Cincinnati: University of Cincinnati, 1972), p. 7.

9. Ibid., p. 22.

10. *New York Times*, January 17, 1977, p. 14.

11. William Worthy, *The Rape of the Neighborhoods* (New York: Wm. Morrow, 1976), p. 47; William L. Slayton, *The University, The City and Urban Renewal* (Washington: American Council on Education, 1963), p. 4.

12. Cox Commission, *Crisis at Columbia* (New York: Vintage, 1968), p. 39.

13. *New York Times*, August 30, 1970, p. 50.

14. Ibid.

15. Carnegie Commission on Higher Education, *The Campus and the City* (New York: McGraw-Hill, 1972), p. 83.

16. Ibid.

17. K. C. Parsons, "The Role of Universities in City Renewal," in *Taming Megalopolis*, ed. H. Wentworth Eldredge, vol. II (New York: Anchor, 1967), p. 986.

18. William Deane Smith, "Wayne State University and Its Neigh-

bors" (Detroit: Wayne State University Center for Urban Studies, 1969),
p. 3.

19. Ibid.

20. Ibid., p. 1.

21. Ibid., p. 8.

22. Ibid., p. 2.

23. Cox Commission, *Crisis at Columbia*, p. 41.

24. Ibid., p. 42.

25. Ibid., p. 83.

26. Columbia University, *The Human Uses of the University* (New York: 1969).

27. Urban Research Corporation, *Harvard's Student Strike: The Politics of Mass Mobilization* (Chicago: 1970), p. 13.

28. Ibid.

29. Ibid., p. 14.

30. Ibid.

31. Worthy, *The Rape of the Neighborhoods*, p. 43.

32. Ibid., p. 44.

33. Sheldon Wolin and John Schaar, "Berkeley: The Battle of People's Park," *New York Review of Books*, June 19, 1969, pp. 24-31.

34. Ibid., p. 25.

35. J. Martin Klotscke, *The Urban University and the Future of Our Cities* (New York: Harper & Row, 1966), p. 73.

36. George O. Nash, *The University and the City: Eight Cases of Involvement* (New York: McGraw-Hill, 1973), p. 22.

37. *Who's Who In America 1970* (Chicago: A. N. Marquis, 1970).

38. James Ridgeway, *The Closed Corporation* (New York: Random House, 1968), pp. 216-223.

39. Carnegie Commission, *The Campus and the City*, p. 84.

40. Larry Sawers and Howard M. Wachtel, "Who Benefits from Federal Housing Policies?" in *Problems in Political Economy: An Urban Perspective*, ed. David M. Gordon, 2nd ed. (Lexington, Mass.: D.C. Heath, 1977), p. 504.

CHAPTER 4

The impact of urban studies and urban research

The emergence of urban studies, urban research, and university involvement in the affairs of the city has had limited impact on substantively changing the urban condition. Urban-studies programs are still in the developmental stage. Urban-extension programs, initially sponsored by foundations, have had little meaningful results. Urban research has been hampered by a national policy that curtails much of its effectiveness. In short, urban studies and urban research have still to fully play a significant role in the urban experience.

The rise of urban studies and urban research was long delayed by the agrarian bias in higher education in the nineteenth and early twentieth centuries. The agrarian myth pervaded not only the choice of locations for the colleges and universities but also their curriculum and their orientation. Although the service aspect of the university had been established with the creation of the land-grant colleges and enhanced by the development of state universities, neither of these movements seemed to touch the particular and growing needs of urban populations. The only indication of concern or interest in the urban community was evidenced in the minor forays of a few of the colleges in the field of social work largely through joint efforts with the newly formed settlement houses.

The land-grant colleges had established a significant precedent for the urban university that was virtually ignored. Lacking the basis for a curriculum when they were established, the land-grant colleges experimented for two decades with the development of a program of study, research, and technical service for the farmer. Lacking a clientele eligible for higher education, they moved into the precollege preparation of students, creating their own clients and at the same time forcing the expansion of public secondary education. They lowered standards and radically revised concepts of education to fulfill their role.

One would think that this early experience with rural higher education would have been translated to the new urban character of society. Obviously, the prevailing antagonism to cities and their poor, immigrant populations and the extensive commitment to the farm community were more overpowering influences. The extent of the need and the depth of the problems of cities were certainly well known and explored fully in the muckraking literature of the turn of the century. What was lacking and continued to be a source of conflict was federal aid to the cities of America and their populations. Even the state university systems that grew up in the midwest and far west initially (and some to this day) avoided the major cities in their boundaries. The few commuter colleges available to the growing city populations could hardly provide for the numbers and the kind of education and training suitable to city people. Only those students who could afford to leave home, it seemed, were eligible for reconditioning in the seclusion of the residential country or suburban college.

Servicing a student population was only one aspect of the problem. The resources of the university were not to be directed to the resolution of pressing city problems. College curriculum avoided the distasteful subject of the city. Urban history and economics were not taught extensively until after World War II and only now are being established as viable subjects. As might be expected, the battle to be waged on an urban curriculum involved the historical conflict between the classical educationists, who perceived the college as an intellectual preserve, and the more practical educationists, who considered education as a means to an end.

The first phase of that conflict had entailed the natural scientists struggling with the purists to establish their basic science courses as part of the college curriculum. It is noteworthy that the natural scientists were later to be the strongest defenders of the status quo, viewing their own subject areas as the nucleus of all knowledge and constantly questioning the modern practitioner who sought to adjust the curriculum to more current technology. Ironically, in the

1960s, during the battles on university campuses for a pertinent curriculum with flexibility (such as fewer required courses) and independent study on the undergraduate level, the natural scientists stood fast in resisting change. Obviously, they had long forgotten their own struggle with the classicists in an earlier period.

Although individual courses related to the urban community were adopted in colleges and universities throughout the country over the years, particularly in the social sciences, there have been few programs preparing students in the professions to cope with the problems faced in the cities. After World War I, these institutions were preparing teachers, lawyers, doctors, and so on to enter their professions; they, however, failed to offer training or background related to the special environment of the city. They appeared to avoid the issue of whether any special requirements might be necessary or desirable as a result of urbanization. This may explain in part why, as late as the 1960's, teacher-training institutions had to admit that their courses and practice-training arrangements had to be adjusted to an urban setting. One may venture to suggest that part of the urban crisis itself was caused by this vacuum in education and in the experience of those who were supposed to be solving the problems of the city.

The earlier programs of an urban orientation were in architecture, planning, and social work, and they were astonishingly late in development and elitist in nature. It took two generations of planners to reach an approach to the city that was realistic and concerned somewhat with the poor and the working class. City architecture and planning were predominantly concerned with large buildings, cultural centers, and the total "city-beautiful" concept. This bore little relationship to the housing and recreation needs of the large majority of city dwellers. Perhaps only the settlement-house approach (although pervaded by paternalism) attempted to adjust its institutional goals to the more fundamental character of city people and their needs. The university remained for the most part aloof in its recruitment policies, its programs and curriculum, and in its training of professionals who would work in the cities.

After World War II, the crisis in the cities broadened and interest in the university began to stir. The misperceptions and neglect were obvious when social scientists turned their attention toward the "metropolitan area" and "metropolitan problems," again displaying the long tradition of anti-city attitudes. These analysts did not foresee the rising racial conflicts that were to emerge in the city of the 1960s, and their consideration of larger areas of service extending into suburbia neglected the basic reason for the migration of middle-class whites from the city.

There were a few academicians, however, who began to appreciate the urban problem and some role for the university in coping with the issue. Paul Ylvisaker at the Ford Foundation (the originator of the Ford Gray Areas project, which initiated the concept of community action later adopted in the Economic Opportunity Act) was one of the first social scientists to relate to the tradition of service of the land-grant college. He developed the concept of the urban land-grant institution, approving funding for several large universities to create urban centers for education and service programs. The emphasis for the university, however, was on research with little interest in or commitment to community service.

The only service conceived of was that to the city government—largely in terms of study and consultation with faculty experts. The urban community, the population of the city, was not a target. Ylvisaker had a broader concept in mind, seeking a more constructive role for the university, working directly with some of the community-action programs. That the universities were ill-equipped to assume this task became evident. Their reputations, built on a history of neglect or exploitation of the poor, did not generate confidence with local residents. On the contrary, most colleges and universities were viewed as an integral part of the "establishment." The civil rights struggles and direct action of the late 1950s and 1960s saw the universities hardly up to the task.

The Ford Foundation, under Ylvisaker's guidance, initiated a series of grants in the late fifties to stimulate university interest in urban affairs. The prime purpose of the grants was to furnish university involvement in city affairs, an "urban extension" program, borrowed from the agricultural extension program of the land-grant colleges. These grants also encouraged the development of graduate urban-studies programs and urban institutes or centers producing research. By the late sixties, the Ford thrust shifted mainly to one encouraging urban research. The urban-extension experiment proved too difficult and was dropped.

The first wave of grants from 1959 to 1966, however, was surprisingly directed to universities outside major metropolitan centers—schools with little experience or commitment to urban problems.[1] Eight universities were beneficiaries of these grants totalling $4.5 million: Berkeley, Delaware, Illinois, Oklahoma, Missouri, Purdue, Rutgers, and Wisconsin. Implicit in several of the grant arrangements was the effort by Ford (or more precisely by Paul Ylvisaker) to try to direct the universities into some of the already funded Ford Gray Areas projects. At a minimum, the hope was somehow to encourage university concern with local community problems and to insure the use of university resources for these purposes.

The first Ford grant in the urban-studies area was made to Rutgers University in 1959. Integral to the program was the requirement for establishing a working liaison between the university and governmental agencies. Rutgers created an Urban Studies Center, which handled the $1.25 million in grant funds.[2] The university assembled an interdisciplinary staff with major emphasis on sociology. One of its major efforts for direct community contact was the South Side Project, which sought a center involvement with a low-income area. Largely, however, the university concentrated its efforts on experimental education (in the development of seminars and internship programs) and technical assistance to state and local governments. In the latter effort, the center concentrated on working with the New Jersey Office of Economic Opportunity. Under the leadership of John Bebout, the Rutgers Center focused on converting the agricultural extension idea to an urban orientation. In their original presentation to Ford, the Rutgers group developed their rationale on the Ylvisaker premise that an urban society could effectively use the idea and experience of the land-grant colleges to cope with growing urban issues.

The Berkeley grant of over $200,000 called for the most direct relationship with the Oakland Gray Area project. According to the foundation report, the "University-Oakland Project was designed to speed up the application of university research and services to actual community problems through extension activities tailored to local needs."[3] The grant was to be used to form a three-way link among official agencies, grass-roots organizations, and the university. It certainly seemed reasonable that the resources of the university should be used to facilitate resolution of local urban problems. As might be anticipated, however, the university confronted some of the same difficulties experienced by the Gray Areas projects, that is, conflict with established city agencies. The university quickly established "that relationship with associations and civic organizations should be limited to providing aid for such projects as would not involve active conflict with an agency of city government."[4] The Berkeley-Oakland experience provided a significant insight into the evolution and character of university urban-studies programs.

Although several of the urban centers were committed to direct involvement with grass-roots community organizations, they had to be particularly cautious lest they be labeled controversial. Other universities suffered from their historical role of non-involvement or hostile involvement with their surrounding populations. This citizenry was not necessarily receptive to the new face of the university as a partner. Considering that the large majority of institutions and their faculties had little interest in or desire to work with local communities—after all, contacts and contracts with city agencies were more lucrative and more beneficial to the academician—there were few institutions that moved to a more direct relationship with community groups. Some encouragement was provided by federal funding of local agencies under the poverty legislation as university faculties saw the opportunity for financial gain and possible research projects for their staffs.

Ford grants to the universities of Delaware, Missouri, Oklahoma, Purdue, and Illinois varied only slightly. In each case, a new unit separate from the existing structure was established and the grant was used for a program of limited impact—generally, to provide some service to the community. Missouri, for example, employed a home economist to work in Kansas City and also hired a community-development agent who was later judged ineffective. The Oklahoma money was used to develop urban scientists through an internship program co-sponsored with local chambers of commerce.

At Purdue, Ford funds were used for a family service program and at Illinois, three urban specialists were hired to carry out research.[5]

In its next phase of urban college funding, Ford policy reflected an awareness of the deficiency of its first effort. In 1966, a major grant of $10 million to Columbia University sought greater inter-action between the university and the community. In fact, Columbia was forced to use the money in cooperation with community-action groups in the area to improve conditions and establish viable work-ing relationships and continuing programs. After the first year, Ford officials were disheartened to learn that the bulk of the funds were again being used to establish university chairs and fund academic research. The Harlem community demonstrated its hostile attitude toward the university in a series of protests against the construction of a university gymnasium on the only park site in the area. Not many groups (certainly not the more militant ones) were willing to work with university officials who seemed to have so little regard for their needs.

The confrontations in the sixties between urban universities and student and community activists spurred the Ford Foundation to increased support of urban university involvement. In the five-year period between 1969 and 1974, Ford donated some $30 million to about a dozen prestigious urban universities "to help them hook into the urban scene."[6] Universities such as Harvard, MIT, Colum-bia, and Chicago were the recipients. However, most of these funds endowed about a dozen professorships.

There was a fundamental difference soon apparent in the Ford effort to build an urban interest in the colleges. Although the land-grant college embodied the idea of a whole new curriculum with a practical objective—improving the technology and life of the farmer —the urban grants had no such comprehensive goal; the urban cen-ters were appendages to existing liberal arts institutions. The most celebrated of the urban centers was at Harvard-MIT, which did produce an undersecretary of urban affairs, a counselor to the pres-ident, and some esoteric books. People at the foundation who helped develop these centers generally admitted to their narrow scope and limited role. Few of these centers attempted to change courses in the college undergraduate curriculum, and even fewer were able to reach out to the communities.

The urban effort, aside from its minimal funding, also was largely directed at assisting local governments—its clientele was not the urban resident. There was little effort to develop any body of knowledge that would enhance resolution of urban problems. The Ford grants, particularly in light of the schools selected for funding, seemed to be a minimal prodding to arouse research interests in urban problems, and no more. The fact that Ford was willing to invest its money in separate units of the university is telling in itself. It must have realized that such an arrangement would have little impact on the university itself.

To some degree, the availability of private and public funding became a stimulus to the adoption of urban programs at many institutions. The federal government, responding to the larger social movement of the sixties, gave much money to universities to respond to the unrest in the cities; these funds mainly came from the poverty program, the Department of Health, Education and Welfare, and the Department of Housing and Urban Development. City governments increased their funding to urban universities also. This was readily perceived by the local population and, expectedly, was resented. The university, however, remained unwilling to respond to the immediate needs of this clientele. For the most part, it retained its rigid requirements and standards for admissions and developed few programs for preparing or servicing this population that so desperately needed credentials and an educated background to become active participants in the city. The commitment to defend the existing city power structure added to the limited role the university could play.

All in all, the relatively planned effort by Ford to strengthen university interest in urban affairs had severe drawbacks. It resulted in some cases in the recruitment of faculty and, at best, an initial foray into the community. We should learn something, however, from that experience. Any ad hoc effort to convert existing colleges and universities to a comprehensive urban program is not to succeed. Reliance on the traditional disciplines and expectation that intermingling will produce positive results are unrealistic. Just as in the case of the land-grant colleges, a new curriculum and a dedication to knowledge that will deal with urban problems as a whole are essential. This is likely to take a good deal of experimentation and years of effort by many people, and the foundations have given us little insight into this area.

The major problem of the urban-studies programs developing in the late sixties and seventies—besides credibility—had been to establish autonomous departments, rather than remain subspecialities within the existing traditional departments. Urban studies confronted the traditional hostility of established academic departments much in the same fashion as had American Studies in the 1950s and later black, ethnic, and women's studies in the 1970s. Part of that problem has been the suspicion of any interdisciplinary program, and part has had to deal with a fuzziness over the parameters of urban studies. In the first issue of *Urban Affairs Quarterly* in 1965, urbanist David Popenoe raised the issue: "What is the focus of the field of urban studies and what are its boundaries. . . . ?"[7] A decade later, the same question would still be pertinent. William C. Pendelton of the Ford Foundation, reviewing his organization's urban commitment, would ask, "What is urbanism as a field of study?"[8] The question was not rhetorical. Much confusion arose over the nature of urban studies, and whether these programs could claim areas that were formally considered subspecialities within traditional academic disciplines. Pendelton seriously queried the thrust of urban studies at the 1974 annual meeting of the Council of University Institutes for Urban Affairs. He shocked the participants by stating that ". . . all of our eggs should not be put into the urban studies basket . . . the best research on urban problems is likely to be done by the good economist, the good political scientist, the good sociologist. . . ."[9] The first urban center director, John Bebout, at the 1976 annual meeting of the council would muse in retrospect that for urban studies, "the identity problem will not go away" and that "the status of urban studies in the university will continue to be in flux."[10]

By the late seventies, there were several hundred urban-studies programs throughout the nation organized in departments and in some as schools in both undergraduate- and graduate-level programs—with fifty universities granting masters degrees and a few granting Ph.D's.[11] But that was not accomplished without some serious misgivings in academic quarters. Sociologist Andrew M. Greeley struck "a word of caution" about "the new urban studies."

Foremost, Greeley warned, the new field should have "*educational*" goals. Greeley hoped that the turmoil of the sixties would not make urban studies "merely a response to guilt feelings, merely an attempt by the college to 'do something' about the inner city . . . [or] they are probably doomed before they start."[12]

Most urban-studies programs were a blend of social science disciplines: economics, sociology, history, education, planning, political science—all from an urban perspective. In essence, these urban-studies programs sought to imitate their traditional academic rivals. Some, however, opted for experimentation in the land-grant tradition. Dr. Marilyn Gittell of Queens College, City University, for example, devised an urban-studies program in the early seventies that disregarded traditional admission procedures and sought candidates in the masters program whose committment to social involvement preceded academic grades. In a number of cases, students in the masters program were admitted without a bachelor's degree, but with significant urban work experience. In addition, the program was heavily involved in field experience and independent study.

But the field of urban studies was not without its critics. Some, like sociologist James H. Huber, felt that urban studies was still a bogus area. Moreover, urban studies was seen to be more a part of the problem than a part of the solution. "As was the situation with the March of Dimes," Huber wrote, "urban studies may inevitably result in the continuances of the urban problem, rather than in its solution."[13] Huber seriously questioned the assumptions of urban studies. Among these assumptions were an uncritical acceptance of the urban crisis and the belief that this crisis can be solved through rational social science efforts best organized under the umbrella of urban studies. Huber doubted the severity of the urban crisis and doubted whether public policy could basically alter the urban condition. Revealing his academic traditionalism, he thought that anything urban studies could do could be done just as well in the regular academic disciplines.

The crucial assumption, as Huber pointed out, is whether there is an urban crisis. Advocates of urban studies and urban research, of course, predicated their arguments on that assessment. Critics, such as Huber and Irving Kristol, were less inclined to agree. Perhaps the most celebrated and extensive polemic challenging the idea of an urban crisis was contained in Edward Banfield's *The Unheavenly City*. Banfield's main line of reasoning was that the problems in the urban crisis were "important in the sense that a bad cold is important, but they are not serious in the sense that a cancer is serious."[14] These problems, mostly dealing with urban poverty, are "relative," and, more important, "are really conditions that we either cannot change or do not want to incur the disadvantages of changing."[15]

What Banfield assumed, in turn, was that poverty essentially was of one's own making; that is, that one was poor due to the inability (or unwillingness) to conceive a future and to plan and defer gratification for that future. "Lower-class poverty . . . ," he wrote, "is 'inwardly' caused (by psychological inability to provide for the future, and all that this inability implies)."[16] Consequently, the public policy cannot, in the final analysis, affect the outcomes, since the fault lies not with the system but with ourselves.

Many commentators have scored this analysis as being grossly inaccurate. They cited the fact that Banfield had wholly neglected the historic and current discrimination against the poor, especially the black poor.[17] They questioned his assumption that deferred-gratification patterns exist only for the middle class and upwardly mobile. (William Ryan cited a study where poor people responded that they would primarily save money that had been given them as a windfall).[18] But, most important, Banfield's assumption of the poor living only for the moment was one concocted from the confines of a study with little evidence to substantiate it. What evidence we have suggests that the poor live for the moment not out of laziness, but out of hopelessness from a life spent in marginal employment with little skills for advancement and little opportunity for higher education. That is the conclusion of the famous participant-observation study in the urban ghetto of Washington, D.C., made by Eliot Liebow in the mid-sixties.[19] It corroborated other studies that pointed to a "real" urban crisis.

Preceding the large-scale development of urban-studies programs and departments were urban-research institutes. Spurred by the growing urban concern in the sixties, new institutes were created, often on the initiative of enterprising academics. By the mid-seventies, there were some 300 urban institutes in universities throughout the United States, a remarkable increase from the 80 that existed in 1967.[20] As these institutes began to proliferate, a number of urbanists, led by Professors Bert Gross of Wayne State University and Warner Bloomberg, Jr., of the University of Wisconsin, organized a Council of University Institutes for Urban Affairs in 1969. In a preliminary meeting held in March of that year, about half of the directors of the urban institutes met to initiate procedures to organize a national council and to discuss mutual concerns. Chief of these concerns was the research-action role of the institutes, a topic that proved "the most 'controversial' of all the sessions."[21] The concept of action research, or advocacy research, was the most pressing in the formative years of the urban institutes. The discussion was on the "constraints upon centers," involving both institutions and clients, and "the fuzziness and lack of clarity over the action role of centers."[22] The debate over action advocacy research was continued in the founding meeting in Boston that fall over how far the urban institutes could serve establishment interests, which in most cases meant prevailing local government. The second concern at the founding conference was the ability to obtain credentiality in the form of undergraduate and graduate degree-giving departments. The debate carried over to next year's first annual meeting of the council, where keynoter Professor Gross wondered whether the urban studies centers were "facades or change agents."[23]

The question of advocacy research was troublesome. H. Paul Friesema openly discussed in the *Urban Affairs Quarterly* the dilemma of serving established interests. The chief problem with advocacy research, he argued, was that "the academics interested in municipal government became captured and coopted (no doubt willingly) by the clients they cultivated. . . ."[24] Equally important, he felt that advocacy research was, in the final analysis, thin in providing solutions to deep-seated problems, and that "more fundamental and theoretical questions are easily deferred."[25]

Yet, the problem of advocacy research is crucial to the effectiveness of urban centers designed for meaningful change. Unfortunately, the tendency in academia has been exclusively toward basic research, with the bulk of social science efforts involved with attitudinal studies, many of which give less than accurate representations, and all of which have little importance in determining public policy. However, policy-geared research seeks to make substantive changes within our society. The trouble with the universities in the urban-affairs field is not that they have had too much advocacy research but that they have had too little.

Part of the problem of too little advocacy research has been due to the very nature of research efforts. Few community groups interested in social change have been able financially to sponsor advocacy research at the urban universities. On the other hand, established interests, especially in local government, not necessarily enamoured of sweeping change, have had the financial resources. Consequently, much research on the university level has tended to be on behalf of the status quo.

Moreover, the very financial structure of urban-research centers is precarious. Most urban institutes depend for a large share of their funds—others depend for a significantly large share—on foundation and government contracts rather than institutional support from their universities. Although the urban universities are eager to have these institutes for both the prestige and financial overhead they bring to the university, they are either not so ideologically committed to the institute or not financially in a position to help. The trouble with foundation and governmental funding is that it is short-lived. Foundations have operated under the premise that funding be only in terms of "seed" money that will launch a program; permanent funding must come from other sources. In that fashion, the foundation envisions itself in its role of stimulating ideas within the society. Unfortunately, that has forced the urban-institute director constantly to hustle for funds. In the recession of the seventies. where even such large foundations as Ford have had their endowment of $3 billion reduced to $2 billion through poor return on investments, the foundations have found it necessary to cut back their grants, with the result that a number of urban institutes went out of operation.

More important, national policy has limited severely the role of advocacy research in these institutes. In the Tax Reform Act of 1969, Congress prohibited foundations from encouraging any attempts to influence legislation through influencing public opinion.

What that meant was that research that was foundation funded could make no recommendations for public policy that would concern changing any specific legislation. That law was the result of the Ford Foundation efforts in the sixties that engendered controversy over two of its social experiments. The first involved the battle over community control and school decentralization in New York City, which ignited racial hostilities; and the second was funding the Congress of Racial Equality's voter registration drive in Cleveland, which encouraged black voters to elect the city's first black mayor. The congressional reaction to foundations possibly influencing constituents and legislatures was to curtail the activities of the foundations in promoting social change—all of which served as constraints on the urban centers in the direction of their policy research.

Professor C. Harold Brown, chairperson of the Council of University Institutes for Urban Affairs, would wonder in the fall of 1976: "Whatever happened to the 'urban crisis?' "[26] Since the student and community protests of the sixties had abated under the forces of an economic recession and conservative public policy, the urban institutes were more involved with credentiality—what Brown called "the extent to which urban programs fit the 'central mission' of the institution," which "gets interpreted as the development of degree programs and rank and tenure for the faculty."[27] Indicative of this approach was the "five-year project in community involvement" of The George Washington University, sponsored by a Mellon grant, that was hailed as "a new direction for the urban university."[28] The "new direction" mainly consisted of extending urban-studies courses.

The most comprehensive studies of the history of higher education in America have concluded that few efforts to change the university have borne fruit. Institutional change is usually accomplished by adding new institutes or programs, bypassing the existing structure. In fact, new colleges are created to carry forth new educational ideas. This was true of the progressive education movement that spawned Swarthmore, Bennington, Antioch, and Oberlin; it was also true of the service concept that was the theme of the land-grant colleges and state universities.

With this experience of resistance to change on the part of the older colleges and universities, it would seem apparent that efforts to expand the concept of urban education should have immediately been translated into a new form of college. The creation of the urban institutes was a gesture to make change in existing institutions, but their limitations makes it even more obvious that any effort to develop a concept of an urban college requires the creation of new institutions. The existing colleges and universities can then continue to function in their own style and not feel threatened by these radical new concepts of education. One of the most important aspects of American higher education, perhaps its major contribution, is the diversity of institutions developed over the years. The urban college can be yet another step in this direction.

NOTES

1. Ford Foundation, *Urban Extension* (New York: Ford Foundation, 1966), p. 1.

2. Ibid., p. 15.

3. Ibid., p. 24.

4. Ibid., p. 25.

5. Ibid., pp. 20-35.

6. William C. Pendelton, *Urban Studies and the University: The Ford Foundation Experience* (New York: Ford Foundation, April 1974), p. 7.

7. David Popenoe, "On the Meaning of 'Urban' in Urban Studies," *Urban Affairs Quarterly* 1, no. 1 (September 1965): 65.

8. Pendelton, *Urban Studies*, p. 9.

9. Council of University Institutes for Urban Affairs, *Communication* IV, no. 4 (March 1976): 3.

10. John E. Bebout, "Urban Studies: Retrospect and Prospect," *Urban Affairs in Transition* (Atlanta: Council of University Institutes for Urban Affairs, 1976), p. 50.

11. Sherman M. Wyman, "Key Dimensions for Urban Affairs Master's Degree Curricula," *Urban Affairs in Transition* (Atlanta: Council of University Institutes for Urban Affairs, 1976), p. 26.

12. Andrew M. Greeley, "The New Urban Studies—A Word of Caution," *Educational Record*, Summer 1970, p. 236.

13. James H. Huber, "Urban Studies: An Opportunity for Synthesis Among Social Policy Sciences," *Intellect* 104, no. 2369 (November 1975): 164.

14. Edward Banfield, *The Unheavenly City* (Boston: Little, Brown, 1970), p. 6.

15. Ibid., p. 5.

16. Ibid., p. 13.

17. Raymond S. Franklin and Solomon Resnick, *The Political Economy of Racism* (New York: Holt, Rhinehart & Winston, 1973), p. 169.

18. William Ryan, *Blaming the Victim* (New York: Pantheon, 1971), p. 127.

19. Eliot Liebow, *Tally's Corner* (Boston: Little, Brown, 1967).

20. Pendelton, *Urban Studies*, p. 3.

21. Conference of Urban Study Center Directors, "University Urban Studies Centers—Observations from Within," March 27-29, 1969, Wayne State University, Detroit, Michigan, p. 51.

22. Ibid.

23. Council of University Institutes for Urban Affairs, *Proceedings of the First Annual Conference* (Washington: 1970), p. 6.

24. H. Paul Friesema, "Urban Studies and Action Research," *Urban Affairs Quarterly* 7, no. 1 (September 1971): 6.

25. Ibid., p. 5.

26. *Communication* V, no. 2 (September 1976): 5.

27. Ibid.

28. *Communication* IV, no. 6 (May-June 1976): 2.

The controversy over black studies

In a significant fashion, black studies relates to the urban experience. For one thing, a large majority of blacks have lived in cities since World War II. For another thing, most blacks attend urban colleges.[1] The most comprehensive assessment of black studies showed that a majority of these programs are at urban universities.[2] Moreover, scholarly analysis of the city often means analyzing the black experience; study of urban poverty, for example, essentially, is a study of black poverty. In short, the black experience, in recent years, has been an urban experience.

The controversy over black studies has been unique in the history of American education. Few innovations occasioned such heated response. Certainly, the urban-studies thrust and later women's studies and ethnic studies did not trigger the reaction that black studies had. The controversy over black studies indicated the singular degree of racial division in this country and especially in the universities. Although there were a few black-studies programs in the black colleges as early as the 1920s, black studies essentially erupted on the scene as a major educational force with the student protests of the mid-sixties, which coincided with a shift in emphasis of the black rights movement from integration to black power.[3] In its first phase of emergence in the late sixties, black studies was the center of a national storm and received considerable attention from the mass media and serious and scholarly journals. By the mid-seventies, the national controversy had faded and the antagonism to black studies shifted from a national to an institutional setting.

Blacks had equated academic equality primarily with obtaining black studies. They had been less concerned with the quantitative

—open admissions, special remedial courses, free tuition, and the like—and more preoccupied with the qualitative—the acceptance and recognition of one's blackness. This psychological truth was the main legacy of the Black Power movement.

The social sixties offered one crucial insight into equality. This idea, whose time had come, had once been considered, dismissed, and forgotten; instead, a myth of equality took shape that merely clouded reality. Generations since the Great Depression grew up clinging to the myth of a melting-pot America. Equality in America, the schoolbooks had it, meant assimilation, integration, acculturation. Growing up in America was understood as the shedding of old origins, pasts, and identities and the taking up of new origins, pasts, and identities.

Nothing was further from the truth. America, we discovered, was not a melting pot, one large amalgam alchemizing peoples as Nathan Glazer and Daniel P. Moynihan argued in their book *Beyond the Melting Pot* in the early sixties. At best, we were a pluralistic society of well-organized and powerful sets of subcultures. Our strength as a nation and the strength of the individual American lay in emphasizing the cultural differences within the wider matrix of the abstraction called Americanism. So sociologists discovered a paradox of difference within unity in their study of ethnic groups. Sociologists Andrew Greeley and Peter Rossi, in their study of Catholics and their schools, *The Education of Catholic Americans*, reiterated the same truth: that the ethnic, racial, and religious subcultures tend to function as healthy shapers of individual and collective identities.

One best affirmed one's identity by acknowledging one's subculture. One could conceive of a Frenchman, an Italian, or a German as part of a distinct homogeneous group with a wider reference as European. Similarly, one was black, French, Irish, or Jewish within a stronger reference as American.

The black movement of the mid-sixties must be credited with resurrecting the concept of identity. The Civil Rights movement inevitably moved from its paternalistic stage of integration to black awareness and the rise of group consciousness. It was a measure of the depth of racism in America that this simple group journey—a journey traveled by other ethnic groups—would be so reviled and discredited by a large, white, moderate majority. We witnessed the opposition of black power by those conservative and liberal intellectuals who ironically glorified in their own way their particular ethnic group. The editors of the Jewish liberal magazine *Commentary* would regularly dismiss black power as an aberration, yet be strengthening the positive cultural Jewish ambience.

Black power directed attention to one's identity. One watched the triumphs and failures of black power, while strengthening one's own particular white ethnic identity. Other protest movements such as women's liberation borrowed liberally not only tactics of the Black Power movement but their thought grooves as well.

The search for equality, then, in American life no longer meant becoming one of them: It meant becoming one of us. The key idea and key word was identity. Ironically, the most socially conscious of American history concluded that the problems of the "We" boiled down to a problem of "I". This hallmark psychological truth permeated all areas of American life in the social sixties. Not only did women's liberation groups seek to redefine the image of women by women, but homosexual groups stressed the pride of being different, as did ethnic groups.

Equality in American life for the blacks first meant a change of psychology. No longer could the whites dominate the game and make up the rules as they saw fit. Black power essentially meant that the blacks could make up their own definitions and their own rules; the first of these was to declare their independence from the white world by ceasing to hate themselves and their blackness and by glorying in their difference. That signified creating a usable past. The most oppressed of Americans sought the first qualitative step towards a new equality by creating this usable past called black studies.

The emphasis on identity has not abated during the seventies. Instead, it has continued to permeate the social, cultural, and political fabric. Nearly all ethnic and minority groups have stressed their heritage. The black experience has been continuously plumbed with great interest. In 1977, journalist Alex Haley's geneological search for his black heritage in America and Africa proved to be an unparalleled media event: Haley's book, *Roots,* became a leading bestseller in hardcover, and a week-long television serialization proved to be the most watched show in the history of television. The concern with identity and heritage was still strong.

Black studies initially proliferated at an unbelievable rate. Seven states immediately passed laws requiring some form of black studies in secondary school curricula and six other states issued policy statements through their state boards of education and state departments of education.[4] A Spelman history professor, Vincent Harding, established a national center for black studies in Atlanta— Institute of the Black World—servicing black-studies programs at various colleges, and later a National Council on Black Studies was formed.[5] In addition, the interest in the black experience produced two new scholarly journals: *Black Scholar* and the *Journal of Black Studies*. The demand for black Ph.D.'s for professorial positions and black-studies chairmanships became widespread.

College adminstrators, in turn, blunted their responses to make the university pertinent to the needs of a black urban poor mainly by agreeing to institute some black-studies programs. A sample survey revealed that approximately two-thirds of college and university administrations felt "that a special course emphasizing the contributions of Negroes to the culture of the United States would be advantageous in easing racial tension."[6] This response was enlightening when one considers that 84 percent of these institutions reported less than 10 percent of their student body as being black. Over two-thirds of black students, according to a study by the Urban Research Corporation, felt that the urgent need on American campuses was for a black-studies program.[7] Of the 292 student college protests in 1969, 49 percent were for black recognition of some kind, and the most insistent demand (32 percent) was for more black courses or black studies. This latter demand even dwarfed that of increasing the number of black students on campus (24 percent).[8]

The black-studies movement reached a peak in 1971. That year there were some 500 schools offering majors in black studies. Three years later that number would dwindle to 200, and by 1977 there would be an increase to 300, with a half-dozen universities, including Harvard, offering master's degrees.[9] No university has yet offered a Ph.D. in black studies but advocates hope that doctoral programs are not too far in the future. Many black students, worried primarily over future careers in the recession of the seventies, lost interest in black studies. By the mid-seventies, there was a decline in student enrollment in these programs, although half of the colleges and universities were offering some courses on the black experience. Enrollment has remained overwhelmingly black.

Black studies loomed largest at two nationally covered campus confrontations in the late sixties, both at San Francisco State, the first college to conceive a black-studies curriculum, and Cornell University, the first major American university to adopt black studies. White and black students and faculty became embroiled in hostilities largely over the administration of an Afro-American curriculum.

At Cornell, the dispute reached a dramatically frightening point: Black bandoliered students armed with rifles had occupied a building. There was the usual black tokenism syndrome at Cornell that led to a long series of events in preparation for open confrontation. A small number of black students had been added to the less than 20 in 1964 so there were more than 250 in the university by 1968. The university had neglected its social role in the surrounding urban ghetto and had hoped to escape black activism with its "pioneering" program of recruiting black high-risk students. A sympathetic *New York Times* editorial reinforced false feelings of security on the part of university administrators that they were in the lead in seeking poor black students.

Nevertheless, trouble was visible early. Blacks were resentful of being excluded from white fraternities. They turned inward and demanded all-black housing on campus. Their priority, however, was for the creation of an Afro-American studies program. By the fall of 1968, Cornell agreed to a tentative program. But by the spring term impatient black militant students escalated demands for a College of Afro-American studies with a separate budget. President James Perkins, a liberal academician, reacted strongly to the demand for a full-blown black studies college.

If any college is to be part of Cornell University—carry the Cornell name, recommend to me and the trustees candidates for faculty with Cornell status and those courses which are to receive credit for a degree —then the autonomy you describe is impossible.[10]

A series of minor clashes, empty rhetoric, demonstrations, and student takeovers culminated in white and black threats and the appearance, for the first time, of students with rifles. A four-foot cross was set ablaze a la Ku Klux Klan in front of a black women's cooperative shortly after three black students were mildly reprimanded for disruptive activities. Some eighty black students then occupied Willard Straight Hall and eventually armed themselves through couriers.

President Perkins temporarily resolved the impasse by agreeing to rescind the reprimands and reconsidering student demands on black studies. President Perkins' actions were later challenged by the faculty, which voted by more than two to one (726 to 281) to punish the three black students. After considerable administrative pressure, the faculty reversed its decision, fearing more serious campus unrest. What is particularly instructive is that the administration, although somewhat resistant to student participation in policymaking, was much more liberal and flexible than the faculty.

The lesson of the San Francisco State College confrontation, however, was one of repression. It gave national prominence to an educator, Professor S. I. Hayakawa, as a symbol of reaction at a time when most of the liberal educators had been found inadequate to deal with student rights. At San Francisco State, the administration had hired a nationally known black sociologist, Dr. Nathan Hare, recently dismissed from Howard University for his militancy, to head a new black-studies program. Again, black student demands escalated from a program to a degree-granting, all-black department in black studies. The strike that ensued over disciplining students for a demonstration toppled one university president and gave rise to Hayakawa and the emphasis on law and order.[11] These events helped to unleash a wave of anti-student feeling.

How had blacks perceived black studies? Initially, those like Dr. Nathan Hare, the former interim chairman of the Department of Black Studies, San Francisco State College, conceived of black studies as educational in thrust: "Two key functions of black studies are building ego-identity and ethnic confidence for the black student," he said in a special report of the National Education Association.[12] "The major motivation of black studies is to entice black students (conditioned to exclusion) to greater involvement in the

educational process. Black studies is, above all, a pedagogical device."[13] A black moderate, Carl T. Rowan, former USIA director,
challenged the idea of black studies: "Black studies," he said,
"should be for whites, not blacks. Any black who majors in that
study ought to have his head examined."[14]

A differing black view, one that surely represented the majority
of black opinion, was expressed by Vincent Harding when he considered black studies as being something more than an educational
approach, one that has political and social bearing. "Many of us
see black studies as part of a struggle," Harding said. "American
education has been set up to proclaim the goodness of American
society. All education has been used for the community it is part
of. It is perfectly legitimate to use black studies as a service to the
black community."[15]

The latter concept had fueled the almost unequivocal support
black students and black spokesmen have initially given the black-
studies movement; black studies had become a litmus test to determine the university's commitment to social change. White opposition in the ivoried academic tower merely confirmed for black
America its worst suspicions. Writing in the first issue of a black-
studies journal, *The Black Scholar*, Eldridge Cleaver succinctly
posed the problem: "Our struggle to gain Black Studies Departments on college campuses, our struggle to have black studies
added to the curriculum across the nation is a struggle that the
enemy sees as a grave danger"; this is a condition that has arisen,
Cleaver concluded, because "in the compartmentalized thinking of
the traditional American society, the college community and the
college campus is viewed as something separate and distinct from
the rest of the community."[16]

Clearly, the position of black-studies advocates (and it cannot be
overly stressed that with a few notable exceptions they were black)
had been to hold the university accountable for its gross intellectual
neglect of black people. In sum, black-studies advocates called both
black and white institutions of higher learning to task to expiate
their guilty pasts. In a trenchant article on black studies, black sociologist Gerald McWhorter in *Black Studies and the University* em-
phatically accused the university of an historic benign neglect:

... the university has systematically excluded black people—systematically excluded them in admissions, systematically excluded them in devising standards of evaluation that have nothing to do with the styles of life and the indigenous culture of the black community. . . .[17]

This condition was the by-product of the white belief, reinforced, that black as blacks do not exist but are merely shadows, extensions, of the white man, what Whorter called the Myrdalian dilemma:

... the book by Gunnar Myrdal, *An American Dilemma* . . . contains the white Myrdalian dilemma, not the dilemma of black people . . . he saw black people basically the same way as William Faulkner, the white racist novelist of the South. That is, he said that white people presented all of the alternatives available to black people, and if one ever wanted to understand black people, you merely had to look at white people who were around them, calculate the obverse of what you saw and you'd come up with what black people are about. There was no inkling in his mind that over a period of time black people could create a community, a culture, that would be functionally autonomous from the white oppressors who raped them from Africa.[18]

The aim of black studies, then, was to redress this white exclusionary vision.

By the mid-seventies, blacks were reassessing the thrust of black studies. S. Jay Walker, chairman of the Black Studies Program at Dartmouth, felt that black studies had entered a second phase where there was a "weeding out of many programs" and the result was that "the survival only of the fittest, is about to begin."[19] Nevertheless, Professor Walker believed that it would be a mistake to upgrade black-studies programs into departments. Most important, Walker argued that the primary purpose of black-studies programs was no longer to make black students aware of their identity but to have them "develop into black scholars."[20] Another cautious reassessment was made by Theresa R. Love, who considered that black studies should be joined with ethnic-studies programs, and that "a moratorium be placed on ethnic studies as a major" field of academic concentration.[21]

On the other hand, a long-time student of black studies, Nick

Aaron Ford, deplored the merging of black and ethnic studies. Moreover, his concept of the function of black studies was greatly expanded from that of Walker. Black studies should not only continue to emphasize black identity, Ford argued, but they should have wider educational and social objectives: "the radical reformation of American education" and "to train black students in the philosophy and strategies of revolution as a prelude to black liberation."[22]

Another aim of black studies, Ford observed, was preparation for career opportunities. The economic recession of the seventies had affected student majors, so both black and white students were concerned more about preparation of marketable careers. Consequently, black-studies advocates were notably defensive about the value of their programs. Dr. Bertha Maxwell, chairperson of the National Council of Black Studies, emphasized the new stress on career opportunities in black-studies programs. "Black studies programs are now concerned with careers, with developing necessary skills to become marketable," she said. "We must look at the total educational process. We are past the sixties emphasis on black awareness."[23]

The response—both black and white—to black studies had been far more complex than just that of an outright challenge to its legitimacy. Traditionally, white universities and colleges often looked upon black studies as the lesser of two evils, a substitute for social equality. The traditional black colleges, which have functioned as black institutions pursuing white knowledge, feared the black brain drain from their colleges; black studies and black professors, their administrators felt, belonged on their campuses. Black moderates were anxious and unsure of the effects on the possible future integrated society. White moderates, for the most part, were anxious over the tempo of black demands, if not overtly opposed from subdued racist feelings.

An intricate and heated controversy arose over the legitimacy of black studies in the late sixties. One naturally suspected the impulse to create a valid usable past within the American university that is timely and relevant. Yet, most academic innovations were topical. They have, however, flourished with the blessing of the academy because they were free from national social implications, and as such provoked little fanfare. Black studies had been in the eye of a national storm. Laymen wrote long, scholarly letters to such papers as the *New York Times* ridiculing the creation of Swahili courses in public schools as ludicrous, all the while unaware that these same schools offered such exotic languages as Hebrew and Gaelic. Scholars questioned the gross politicalization on the campus in creating black studies as a dilution of academic standards, all the while overlooking the American studies programs that proliferated in the Cold War fifties creating a chauvinistic usable past. Interestingly, there are striking parallels between American studies and black studies: both are interdisciplinary; both seek to imbue their students with strong identities; both have been criticized as being little more than cocktail party curriculums; both reflect the university's adapting to the current social needs; and both have been created in an academic age that is becoming increasingly specialized. Here the similarities end: American studies was proved acceptable in a nation committed wholly to Cold War policies; in most colleges, the most academically advanced students were recruited. On the other hand, black studies had few white professionals or intellectual supporters. The journals of opinion had overwhelmingly printed critiques from white professors.

For the most part, the critics of black studies, hostile in intent, initially challenged the idea of black studies from a reference point that revealed their special point of view. It must be noted in this respect that these critics (including the blacks among them) published wholly in journals with a predominantly white, moderate readership—a publishing establishment, however, ranging from the *New York Times Magazine* with more than a million readership to the smaller magazines such as *The Atlantic*—and a publishing establishment that exerts a considerable influence on public opinion beyond the mere number of subscribers. This is mentioned simply because the debate on black studies was mostly *ad hominem*, with critics appealing at worst to the unspoken racist impulses of their white readers, and advocates of black studies writing in black journals appealing to the racial solidarity of their black readers.

Three main serious arguments were raised against black studies.

First, whites and blacks considered black studies not so much as ego-building tonic as reverse racism that would further polarize the races. If black studies were to be created at all, they should be aimed at further proselytzing the white mind, these integrationists maintained. Second, some white radical critics intoned that black studies were ill-conceived since there could not be intellectually or ideologically a black point of view; rather, the dominant factor in American life was class, and race was but a subdivision of class and not a separate factor. Third, black studies were considered unintellectual, cheap palliatives to camouflage the real need to give blacks educational remediation.

The integrationist argument that black studies should be designed for whites involved a piety that no longer held true in American life. That piety was that social change would come about through an appeal to the white conscience. Whites would best benefit from knowledge of the black experience, would be uplifted, and would eventually be provoked to accommodate black demands. No mention was made in this argument of the strengthening of black identities that need to overcome historic self-hate. Rather, black studies became an extension of black power, a "fantasy" of separatism that implied the most dreadful racism.

Let us follow the logic of Kenneth Clark, the black integrationist psychologist, writing in *The Antioch Review*. Black studies, according to Clark, at best, should be for "whites [who] need to face with a terrible honesty the consequences of their own inheritance."[24] Moreover, the separatism of black studies ideologically impedes an integrated society, thus unwittingly abetting those white racists opposed to integration. "Is it required of blacks," Clark continued, "that they . . . identify with the oppressor, collaborate in the efficient implementation of his goals, and rationalize this surrender of spirit and integrity as a realistic adaptation?"[25]

Clark, however, missed the point of black studies: the ego builder. Consequently, he could not appreciate the rebuttal of black Amherst student Stephen Lythcott in *The Antioch Review* to the charge that white consciences be the object of the studies: "For a white student to be in any of these sessions would only blunt the knife, and inhibit fundamental emotions from being expressed."[26] Black studies, then, is partially group therapy. It is a sanctuary where blacks can escape from the dominant white intellectual culture to regroup in "black-consciousness programs," there to find "launching pads for attacks on the system and the society."[27]

More fundamentally, what is wrong with imbuing oneself with the positive aspects of one's group's culture? Black studies, and for that matter, black power, does not negate integration, but merely postpones integration until that group more fully can compete and be free from dominance, benevolence or whatever. For these integrationist critics, however, such an objective is denied the blacks, although permitted for Irishmen, Jews, and Italians. The blacks are "extremists" and their white supporters, "guilty liberals."

If the integrationists had lost the force of their argument in recent years, the Marxists had not. In fact, the scholarly pendulum had swung once again, and one could estimate that a large group of scholars reflects the "fifty-seven" varieties of Marxism, whereas in the fifties these scholars were overwhelmingly conservative. The established academic view was that class—one's SES (socioeconomic-status) rating—predominates in American life. All else is secondary and contingent.

So the radical white historian, Eugene Genovese, could subtly condemn black studies, and for that matter black militancy, despite his pioneer interest in black militancy, all in the name of class. For those who worship at the economic shrine, race does not exist. "There is no such thing as a black ideology or a black point of view," Genovese wrote in *The Atlantic*, ". . . Discrimination against [blacks] is largely a class question, requiring sober analysis of class structure in America . . . and it is therefore a dis-service to the cause of black liberation to construct a politically opportunist equation that can only blur the unique and central quality of the black experience in the United States."[28]

Genovese was not alone. Past scholarly attitudinal surveys of white opinion revealed that middle-class whites would feel more disposed to "accept" blacks if they were not so wretchedly poor. Much of white, middle-class teachers' low expectations of black poor students could be attributed to a class expectation: the poor, and particularly the black poor, these schoolteachers said, have just not been exposed to the cultural advantages that a middle-class child has and one cannot therefore expect too much of them. Of course, this is a self-fulfilling prophecy.

But would, or have, middle-class whites accepted blacks when the economic conditions are equalized? There is no hard evidence to support these unreliable surveys of guilty whites or the dogma of nineteenth-century Marxism; that is, discrimination towards blacks has appeared to be based less on economics and more on race. Certainly, affluent workers or middle-class professionals have still reacted racistly to middle-class blacks. White reaction to black-power advocates documents this. The difficulty of middle-class blacks finding decent housing in white enclaves further reinforces the concept that race does not conform to the laws of class. Certainly, one cannot so easily define anti-Semitism in terms of class. In fact, there appears to be an inverse relation, so the better the fortunes of the Jewish community, the greater the anti-Semitism.

Moreover, the class analysis certainly holds no sway with blacks. For nearly three-quarters of a century, American white radicals have told their black brothers that their problems were at heart problems of class, of economics. Few blacks have heeded. American Marxists have been unable to attract blacks on the strength of their analysis. Some like Ralph Ellison's hero in *The Invisible Man* converted to the Marxist view only to discover bitterly that it was but another white subterfuge to keep blacks in their place. Tell a black man that his problems do not stem from the fact that he is black but because of the class struggle and he will ignore you. He has a visceral belief that it is his blackness that has kept him down so long. The evidence supports him. One need only consult Leslie Fiedler's brilliant study of the black and white images in our national literature, *Love and Death in the American Novel*, with black being a euphemism for evil and white for good, to see how deeply ingrained racism has been in our collective subconscious.

Most important, the doctrine of class contradicted everyday American reality. It failed to explain deep-seated antagonisms between the white poor and the black poor. It failed to explain why the white poor have not rioted and rebelled whereas the black poor have done these things. These riot-rebellions of blacks transcended the issue of poverty and were firmly imbedded in a social system whose structure is racist.

Much of our academic conceptions of class are based on what historian Richard C. Wade so aptly termed a "false analogy" of ethnic comparisons. Unfortunately, this false analogy had become, as Wade pointed out in *Book World*, the cornerstone of public policy in America toward race: a policy that Daniel Moynihan was aptly to christen "benign neglect." That analogy simply states that blacks in America are but the "newest" immigrants making it in the old, ethnic, immigrant way in this nation. Political scientists such as Edward Banfield, editors such as Irving Kristol, and scholars-turned-politicians such as Daniel Moynihan concurred that the rate of progress for blacks had been phenomenal in recent years and that they were well on their "immigrant" route to social and economic stability barring white backlash because of "irresponsible black militancy." The fact is that blacks were among the first immigrants and are still last in the economic struggle because of race. They were kept down by slavery and racial discrimination while the ethnic minorities quickly bypassed them on the economic ladder. Wade's critique of this false analogy bears repeating:

To expect the oldest immigrants to this country, the blacks, to act like the newest is bad logic; to apply mechanically the experience of one racial group to another is bad history; to base public policy on an unexamined analogy is, to be charitable, an unacceptable risk.[29]

Yet, the conventional wisdom of the academy and government today considers class to account for our society.

The third objection to black studies—that they were unintellectual and cheap substitutes for skill training—was the more difficult to answer. For, in truth, the concept of black studies does flounder on these scholarly shores just as did other interdepartmental approaches such as American studies and general education. One cannot expect survey courses to develop depth in a field, and for all the merits of general education, the academy is moving toward greater specialization. This places black studies at a decided disadvantage. At best, black studies can prepare generalists who do

not want nor further need academic specialization that is so necessary for research and the production of future academicians.

There has developed, however, a bogus argument on the unschol-
arliness of these black courses. Not surprisingly, Bayard Rustin, a
black spokesman prominent in the early integration civil rights days,
branded black studies as "soul courses" not worthy of consideration. An instructive debate developed between Thomas Billings,
the white director of Upward Bound, a federal program to bring
more black students to college, and Daniel Moynihan, the president's aide on urban affairs, in the pages of *The New Leader*, over
Rustin's condemnation of black studies.

Billings addressed his memo to his staff and entitled it an "open
letter to Bayard Rustin." He chided Rustin's description of black
studies as froth with no meaning to the real world. Billings wondered whether "the black experience in America has been 'real,'
sufficiently to make it the stuff of study just as much as the culture
of other ethnic groups."[30] Most important, Billings sensed the importance of black studies as ego builders.

Rustin stated the classic position of those opposed to the Black
Power movement. After quickly characterizing Billings as a guilty
white liberal, Rustin condemned him as one of those whites who

react with unusual enthusiasm to the position of black nationalists,
would romanticize their demands for separatism and self-determina-
tion, and would identify these demands as the position of the "black
community," when, in fact, they represent the views of a small minority of Negroes.[31]

Moynihan merely apologized profusely to Rustin for a government
official, Billings, using his high office to attack a private citizen.

The exchange had more value than a random curiosity in a journal of opinion. It illustrated the heat of the debate and the levels
of government it reached. Most important, it revealed how substantial a largely white, but also black, resistance there had been over
any program that emphasized blackness. That *The New Leader*
thought this exchange of these incidental memorandas of sufficient
interest for publication indicated the gravity of the issue.

By the seventies the controversy had subsided and was no longer of national media interest. Only one notable broadside was heard in the mid-seventies by Professor Ernest Van Den Haag in the pages of the conservative journal of opinion, *National Review*. Van Den Haag elaborated on the charge that black studies were "not needed for, or likely to help in, acquiring the education useful for careers in American society."[32] He acknowledged that black studies had a therapeutic value in changing the self-conception of blacks but believed them, nonetheless, to be "counterproductive." These programs, he found, did not provide blacks "with the tools required to acquire prestige and income in the existing society and to occupy positions of power."[33] In the end, Van Den Haag wrote, blacks would be better off not with black studies but "studies by blacks."

But the controversy over black studies shifted from a national scene to an institutional setting. Black-studies advocates complained that expansion of black-studies programs had been hampered by "institutional racism." The claim of university recalcitrance seemed to be bolstered by the evidence. Professor Wilson Record in the seventies conducted an attitudinal survey on black studies, interviewing some 209 sociologists in 70 colleges who had some competence and reputation in the area of race and ethnic relations. Professor Record's findings showed that a majority of these sociologists were opposed to the idea of black studies: 22 percent were out-and-out hostile, and 30 percent were against the concept of black studies, but accepted them "as here to stay." Only 28 percent embraced black studies a essential.[34]

What can one conclude about the controversy over black studies? For one thing, both advocates and critics overstated their cases. Advocates overestimated the value of black studies, whereas critics underestimated it. It is ironically instructive that ethnic studies, which were created partly as a backlash movement to the black rights struggle, did not ignite the controversy among either academics or the general public that black studies had.

However, the essential question remains: To what degree can black studies be considered intellectual? One must consider both the therapeutic value of black studies in terms of promoting a healthy self-image of blacks and the scholarly value of these programs. If one regards learning partially based on self-image as basically affective and not cognitive, then, black studies could be considered academically little more than encounter sessions in a university setting with course credit. The truth is that educators have not been in agreement on the bifurcation of what is cognitive and affective. When some do acknowledge these Kantian categories, they regard one as unable to exist without the other.

Flowing from this reasoning, the question has been raised why black studies should be made to flourish on college campuses rather than in elementary and high schools. Confirming this contention is the solid empirical evidence that black studies promotes learning in the lower grades. One study of black programs reported that fifth graders showed a remarkable increase in self-image as a result of black-studies programs.[35] Another study showed an extraordinary two-year jump in reading in fifth graders among black students exposed to black-studies programs, even conceived and administered by white Catholic nuns. Why, then should black studies not be presented at more impressionable ages, when the students are theoretically more impressionable? Yet, the identity studies of Erik Erikson claim an identity crisis within the average American in the early twenties, post-collegiate years—impressionable years of final character formation.

One must concede the therapeutic value of black studies, as even some critics such as Professor Van Den Haag have. On the other hand, few critics have considered black studies a truly scholarly discipline. Their arguments have been based on the paucity of black scholarship in the late sixties. "I believe that the black curriculum cannot be created today," Gerald McWhorter wrote, "not the black curriculum and the black university that I'm interested in being a part of. The simple fact is research does not exist when it comes down to the black community."[36] McWhorter's complaint is one that paradoxically strengthens and cripples the black-studies movement: On the one hand, the idea of black studies is to intellectualize the black experience; on the other, so little scholarship initially existed as to make it questionable whether it is much worth the effort. A book, *Race and the Social Science,* attempted to summarize the scholarship on race in the various disciplines only to have most of its white contributors beg off simply because most studies were either concerned with white attitudes on blacks or did not exist (one contributor noted that the *American Political Science Review* had only six articles from 1906 to 1963 with the word Negro in them).[37]

That situation has, to a large extent, been ameliorated. A cursory examination of public and college libraries as well as bookstores reveals that books on the black experience are second only to books on the Jewish experience in America. One bookshop in New York City (Eighth Street Bookshop), for example, published a booklet on paperback offerings in its black-studies section, numbering several hundred books on the black experience in America. The University of Indiana has catalogued 6,000 dissertations since 1945 dealing with black studies.[38] The black rights movement of the sixties triggered a plethora of scholarship that continues, although not as intensely as in the past few years. Moreover, neglected or forgotten black writers of the past have been reintroduced to intellectual perusal.

That scholarly thrust, however, has not been the prime domain of the small number of black scholars. Indeed, one is disappointed to see that the contributions to such journals as *The Black Scholar* almost totally stress the therapeutic aspect of self-image among blacks but little hard social science data on the black experience in America. Certainly, the most important (and most scholarly) book on the black experience recently has been *The Black Family in Slavery & Freedom, 1750-1925* written by a white professor, Herbert G. Gutman, which challenges previous theories on the pathology of the black family, and not *Roots*, written by a black journalist, Alex Haley, which has been seriously undermined as to its credibility. What one must conclude is that black scholars must concentrate more on scholarly pursuits and less on image, and that black studies cannot be the sole prerogative of black scholars.

It seems that the black man is prepared to go beyond the therapeutic value of black studies to search for material to illuminate black problems in America. He has already begun to sense this need and has begun to address himself to more pragmatic goals. Black-studies advocates have painfully realized the limitations of their approach. They have rightly concluded that the black man must solve problems—largely urban—which have become almost inextricably bound with the fate of blacks in America. Some black urbanologists felt that the creation of black studies was not the "confrontation insurance" colleges and universities hoped for. Black students develop a sense of black identity, but are frustrated in helping other blacks in their community problems, largely urban. Some urbanologists believe that black studies and urban affairs serve separate but related functions. There is a growing belief among concerned black scholars that the emphasis increasingly be on urbanology.

There has been some interest in merging black studies with urban studies. Columbia University considered a plan whereby two separate departments would be created to co-exist side by side: an Afro-American Studies Department and an Urban Studies Department. But by 1977, Columbia had only an Urban Studies Department. At Queens College, CUNY, the black-studies program was located, in a somewhat semiautonomous fashion, within the Urban Studies Department. At its sister institution, City College, the black-studies program has a strong urban emphasis. Dr. Leonard Jefferies, Jr., director of the program at City College, felt that it had "affected the whole 'urban mission' of City College."[39] Increasingly, the concerns of both fields will meld.

The academy's scholarly neglect of the black experience has been corrected. The wheels were too far in motion for a move backwards. Scholarly study of the black experience in America will contribute to a greater understanding and concern for the American experiment.

NOTES

1. Interview with Elias Blake, director, Institute for Service to Education, Washington, D.C., June 13, 1977 (Phone).

2. Nick Aaron Ford, *Black Studies* (Port Washington, N.Y.: Kennikat Press, 1973), pp. 191-95.

3. Ibid., p. 48.

4. Education USA Special Report, *Black Studies in Schools* (Washington: 1969), p. 5.

5. *Newsweek*, August 11, 1969, p. 38.

6. Urban Research Corporation, *Student Protests 1969* (Chicago: 1970), p. 5.

7. Ibid.

8. Ibid.

9. *Newsweek*, March 18, 1974, p. 81.

10. Urban Research Corporation, *Guns on Campus: Student Protest at Cornell* (Chicago: 1970), p. 7.

11. Kay Boyle, *The Long Walk at San Francisco State* (New York: Grove Press, 1970).

12. Education USA Special Report, p. 3.

13. Ibid.

14. Ibid.

15. Ibid.

16. Eldridge Cleaver, "Education and Revolution," *The Black Scholar* 1, no. 1 (November 1969): 48.

17. Armstead L. Robinson et al., *Black Studies in the University* (New Haven: Yale University Press, 1969), p. 57.

18. Ibid., p. 60.

19. S. Jay Walker, "Black Studies: Phase Two," *American Scholar*, Autumn 1973, p. 609.

20. Ibid., p. 615.

21. Theresa R. Love, *Possible Directions for Black Studies in American Colleges and Universities* (St. Louis: ERIC Document Reproduction Service, 1974), p. 4.

22. Ford, *Black Studies*, pp. 59-61.

23. Interview with Dr. Bertha Maxwell, chairperson, National Council for Black Studies, May 23, 1977 (Phone).

24. Kenneth Clark, "Black Studies: The Antioch Case," *The Antioch Review*, Summer 1969, p. 147.

25. Ibid.

26. Stephen Lythcott, "Black Studies: The Antioch Case," *The Antioch Review*, Summer 1969, p. 153.

27. Ibid.

28. Eugene Genovese, "Black Studies: Trouble Ahead," *The Atlantic*, June 1969, p. 38.

29. Richard Wade, Review of *The Unheavenly City*, by Edward Banfield, *Washington Post*, April 26, 1970. p. 4.

30. Thomas Billings, "Black Education and White Liberalism," *New Leader*, December 22, 1969, p. 12.

31. Bayard Rustin, "Black Education and White Liberalism," *New Leader*, December 22, 1969, p. 13.

32. Ernest Van Den Haag, "Black Cop-out," *National Review*, August 30, 1974, p. 971.

33. Ibid., p. 972.

34. Wilson Record, "Response of Sociologists to Black Studies," *Journal of Higher Education* XLV, no. 5 (May 1974): 365.

35. Education USA Special Report, p. 4.

36. Robinson, *Black Studies*, p. 60.

37. Irwin Katz, ed., *Race and the Social Sciences* (New York: Basic Books, 1969).

38. *New York Times*, June 19, 1977, p. 38.

39. Ibid.

CHAPTER 6

National policy and the crisis in education

For much of the past generation, national educational policy has been considered from an egalitarian matrix. The aim of federal public policy, starting with the GI Bill of Rights, was to increase the number of students at colleges and universities, a goal that was predicated on the perception of a postindustrial society that required ever-increasing academic preparation for social mobility. By the seventies, that perception was under severe challenge. A number of social science studies attempted to show that education had little effect on reducing inequality. This thesis—coupled with a serious economic depression that also affected higher education—influenced national educational policy to form into a conservative mold. The value of college was unfairly undermined by brute economic forces and misinterpretation of the dynamics of social change.

The policy of universal access to college, surprisingly, almost diverged along political party lines. Democratic presidential figures have advocated, in varying measure, universal access—at least until the fourteenth year—whereas Republican presidential figures have been concerned with a more conservative meritocratic approach emphasizing remedial action, such as student assistance, rather than a blanket policy of universal higher education.

President Truman highlighted the Democratic policy of universal access with his Commission on Higher Education in 1947, which proclaimed a *right* to college and free college education through the fourteenth year. President Johnson privately favored the Truman policy, and former Vice-President Hubert Humphrey in his presidential race made universal education a 1968 campaign pledge.

101

The major thrust of an egalitarian policy in higher education in the twentieth century came with the GI Bill of Rights during World War II. True to its gospel of education, America rewarded its veterans with a Bill of Rights, the first of which was the right to college.

In 1947, President Truman appointed a blue-ribbon panel representing the education establishment to pursue the implications of the GI Bill. In a series of provoking recommendations, the report concluded that the nation must "make education through the fourteenth grade available in the same way that high school education is now available."[1] The commission interpreted the "critical need"' of higher education for all "in the light of the social role" of colleges and universities.[2] It was "obvious" to the members of Truman's commission "that free and universal access to education, in terms of the interest, ability and need of the student, must be a major goal in American education."[3]

But, most important, the commission clearly enunciated a *right* to college. Education, the report intoned, was not only the "biggest and the most hopeful of the Nation's enterprises," it was the "foundation of democratic liberties."[4] Moreover, education was a "birthright." This, the commission report reassured, was nothing less than part and parcel of the "democratic creed" that "assumes [education] to be their [Americans'] birthright; an equal chance with all others to make the most of their native abilities."[5]

The Truman Commission grappled with the problems of deciding who should go to college. Their answer was framed in the egalitarian land-grant tradition: everyone. The commission *conservatively* estimated that nearly half of our population had the mental ability to finish fourteen years of schooling and one-third could be expected to finish college. The commission also noted that a National Resources Report found that 90 percent of our youth should begin high school and 80 percent should graduate, implying that figure as an upper limit for higher education. They offered a program that optimistically would result in having all students who so wished to be in some college by 1960. One generation and seven presidents later, we are still considering that proposition.

Both the Kennedy and Johnson administrations embodied education as a major theme of their poverty programs: nearly every domestic reform program included some educational training. President Johnson and Vice-President Humphrey displayed a reverence for education that only a former schoolteacher and a former college professor possess, by sponsoring more educational legislation than had been enacted in the previous 190-odd years of the republic.

President Johnson was clear about his belief of the economic efficacy of education. He told a group of planners of the poverty program:

This is going to be an education program. We are going to eliminate poverty with education, and I don't want anybody ever to mention income redistribution. This is not going to be a handout, this is going to be something where people are going to *learn* their way out of poverty. [Paraphrased][6]

Moreover, President Johnson had let it be known through his special assistant for education, Douglas Cater, that he privately favored fourteen years of free schooling beyond high school into junior college. In addition to these public rumblings, Johnson made some significant private soundings on the cost of such a venture. In late 1966, a series of highly confidential studies on universal higher education was completed for the president.[7] What prevented Johnson from passing a universal higher education law, of course, was his escalation of the Vietnam War, which consumed most of the federal budget.

Many prominent educators, most notably in the Carnegie Foundation, followed the Truman-Johnson-Humphrey lead, and emphasized, in different recommendations, some sort of universal access. Recommendations to overhaul completely all current federal programs were made in 1968 in the second report of the Carnegie Commission on Equality in Higher Education chaired by Clark Kerr. Although stopping short of a free, open-admissions policy, the Kerr group advanced federal reforms that would enable all high school students who so wished to be in college by 1970; and all students, including those with severe learning disabilities, to be in some college by the end of the century.[8] Carnegie reiterated its recommendations that there be free access to fourteen years of schooling in three subsequent reports (1970, 1971, 1973). States were urged to control low tuition at public universities and private universities were advised not to charge prohibitive tuition.

The crucial assumption of the Truman-Johnson-Humphrey policy was that the nation's economy had changed from a blue- to a
white-collar economy, with diminishing need for factory, farm, and
unskilled labor, and increasing need for workers with academic
preparation. Indeed, some analysts predicted that this new post-
industrial nation would breed a new class no longer based on property but on education. According to them, the avenues of economic
opportunity were closing. Since the mid-1950s, America has ceased
to be an industrial nation with a manufacturing economy capable
of absorbing unskilled, uneducated labor forces. America has become a postindustrial nation with a service economy. Translated,
that means there have been progressively fewer and fewer jobs requiring only manual skills; in the past decade alone, the number
of jobs requiring a minimum of college preparation has grown by
one half. In a few short years, nearly 90 percent of our work
force will be white collar, constituted by three major groups: professional and technical, managerial, and clerical and sales.

The postindustrial society was a service society. A decade ago,
six out of every ten workers were in services, and it was estimated
that by 1980 seven out of ten would be.[9] One out of six workers
is now employed by government. Most important, the two top
categories of employment—professional and technical, along with
managerial, official, and proprietorship—make up one-fourth of
the work force—categories that theoretically call for college
preparation.[10]

There were two differing responses to the emergence of a post-
industrial service society. The egalitarians sought to have policies
that would prepare workers with the most academic background
obtainable. College meant little in the nineteenth and early twentieth centuries when jobs were plentiful in an expanding primitive
industrialism. Indeed, for many who were poor, schooling interfered
with the more urgent task of making a living. But the development
of capitalism, and the increasingly minor role of manufacturing,
changed that picture.

The advocates of meritocracy saw in the postindustrial state the
rise of an educated elite, a "technostructure," which, in effect, would
rule that society. According to this scenario, in this postindustrial

nation, the greatest economic capital no longer consists of natural resources or the tools of manufacturing but technical brainpower, pure and simple. This twentieth-century America is one wherein the technocrat reigns as high priest, determining the shape and direction of policy in both private and public sectors through expertise. John Kenneth Galbraith observed in *The New Industrial State* that in this new economy, power has shifted from capital to organized intelligence, in which effective power of decision (in public and private institutions) is lodged deeply in the technical, planning, and other specialized staff. The aim of higher education, in sum, is to groom this new breed of technocrat to assume his role. The university, according to Daniel Bell, thus stratifies our class structure. In Christopher Jencks' rephrasing of the same proposition in *The Academic Revolution*, one detects a desire for exclusion: "One of the central functions of higher education—along with providing jobs for scholars—is to control access to the middle-class state."[11] In short, the university can be either the facilitator or barrier to economic opportunity, depending on one's concept of the university's function.

For some, then, the postindustrial state should be educationally organized around meritocracy. It is a mind set peculiarly American. What these advocates argue for is deeply conservative and has roots in much of American conservative thought. This meritocracy is not so much concerned with the great majority who do not make it. "Life is unfair to the poor," Christopher Jencks and David Riesman intone, and their "guess is that universal higher education will diminish the economic or social differences among classes a little but not much."[12] The young, brilliant student who survives the meritocratic struggle becomes the technocrat. It is his duty as a professional reformer, one of the annointed, to accept the stewardship of the many for the welfare of all. For others, however, the need was to extend educational opportunity to all.

What both the advocates of meritocracy and universal education overlooked, however, in the new postindustrial state was the devolution of education into mere credentialism. In Professor S. M. Miller's apt phrase, we had become a "credentials society," where the mere possession of a college diploma provided entry to the economy. Critics of the credential society, notably Miller and Ivar

Berg, conceded the necessity of college for mobility, but underscored the misallocation of education and employment. They pointed out that in the rush to confer degrees on students, the purpose of education was lost.

These critics doubted whether there was sufficient relation between education and work. They maintained that the answer to poverty was not *more* education, as educators oversold on education would have us believe. They argued, quite forcefully, that the greatest expansion of jobs in this postindustrial economy market had not been in the high technocrat level requiring greater levels of education but in the middle service category. Most important, these critics maintained that the level of education and the level of work did not match. We were producing an overeducated class of workers who found themselves increasingly dissatisfied with their jobs and thus did not perform as well as less educated workers trained on the job.

Studies have shown that a good proportion of college graduates have been overqualified—"underemployed"—for their work. A survey by the University of Michigan's Research Center estimated that 27 percent of the country's workers were overqualified;[13] another survey by the U.S. Department of Labor placed that figure at 35 percent;[14] and Myron Clark, past president of the Society for the Advancement of Management, estimated that as many as 80 percent were underemployed.[15]

As Ivar Berg has clearly pointed out, employers have hired on the basis of academic credentials, sifting those with high academic backgrounds, for jobs far below the educational background of the applicant. So young women from prestigious eastern colleges find their college credentials can get them jobs only as secretaries to editors—a clear case of overqualification. As Berg noted, the disparity in pay between a plumber in an effective union and a schoolteacher not in a union is so great that studies have shown those teachers with greater educational preparation are most likely to leave the profession. But the overwhelming argument advanced by persons such as Miller and Berg is that overeducated workers are not as efficient, productive, or personally fulfilled as the less educated worker who has risen from within the ranks of the company.

The implications of these findings might be construed as a strong case against universal higher education. "Given the facts that there are more job openings in the middle, and that many people are overqualified for the jobs they do have," Berg wrote, "policies aimed at upgrading the educational achievements of the low-income population seem at best naive."[16] Instead, Berg felt that what should be done is a massive job upgrading throughout the economy: "It would make better sense to upgrade people in the middle to higher jobs and upgrade those in lower-level jobs to middle positions, providing each group with an education appropriate to their age, needs and ambitions."[17] So the campus, as supporter of the credentials society maintained by the market system, would be abolished.

Critics such as Berg assumed a static economy and, in turn, conceived that employers would cease using academic credentials as a touchstone for hiring, even after a massive on-the-job training program was instituted. Surely, as Berg believed, "in relation to jobs, education has its limits."[18] Nevertheless, the crucial fact remains that the credentials society will not vanish overnight. The likelihood is that employers, still, will hire on the basis of academic background, no matter what retraining policy is pursued.

Nonetheless, critics of the credentials society have struck a responsive chord. Indeed, work and education more often than not are ill-fitted. The fault lies just as much with the college that prepares its clients as with the employer who selects and hires them, or with the larger public that worships at education's shrine. Thus, much of this credentials-society criticism boils down to a critique of college curriculum. For the trenchant question raised by Berg and Miller concerns the aftereffects of overeducation: morale and productivity. This syndrome is more likely to occur in a worker with advanced degrees. Thus, the tendency to overeducation can be said in truth to reach a point of diminishing return. One could therefore propose college as a minimum requirement for all who desire it, and postgraduate work only for those professionals who require the credential. In short, the reforms that logically follow from Berg's inference should be campus reforms. The college should make its curriculum more relevant and the postgraduate school restrict credentialing so far as it can. The answer to overeducation is less education, not more on-the-job training. Moreover, one must realize that the market will tend to correct itself.

The major thrust to the Truman-Johnson policies had been that education provided social mobility. Historically, educators and political leaders had agreed with Horace Mann's axiom that education was the "great equalizer of the conditions of man," which "does better than to disarm the poor of their hostility towards the rich; it prevents being poor."[19] By the seventies, educators and certain scholars were reexamining that proposition. The economic recession of the seventies—with a concomitant oversupply of college graduates who were the youngsters of the World War II baby boom—limited the economic value of a college degree. In concert, a number of studies appeared that questioned whether equality could be achieved through a policy of expanding educational opportunities rather than a policy of equalizing results through some form of income distribution.

The recession of the seventies decreased the economic value of a college degree. The result was a corresponding decline in enrollment in higher education by college-age youngsters: From 1969 to 1976, the proportion of college age youngsters attending college dropped from 44 percent to 33 percent.[20] The mass media were rife with stories of college graduates without jobs. They cited statistics emphasizing the declining economic value of college: The economic advantage a college graduate had in starting salary over other workers dropped from 24 percent in 1969 to 6 percent in 1976; the lifetime income advantage of a college graduate had declined from 11 percent in 1969 to 7 percent in 1974.[21] College, Caroline Bird argued in *The Case Against College*, was the "dumbest investment you can make."[22] Instead, she advised that one would be better off investing the cost of college in a bank.

Graduate education, for the most part, was also severely depressed. There were too many prospective public school and college teachers for jobs: only one job for every two and a half public schoolteaching candidates and only one job for every ten Ph.D. graduates. Professional schools were also overcrowded. There were 45,000 medical school applicants for approximately 15,000 places (over 90 percent of the applicants were academically qualified). Law school applications in a three-year period between 1969 and 1971 increased 116 percent. The most promising occupation was for graduates of business schools with a masters degree in business administration.[23]

Educators were under attack for their egalitarian rhetoric, their academic policies, and their educational aims. They retreated, for the most part, in defense of college in terms of personal values. Indicative of their attitudes was the observation of Harold Howe II, former United States commissioner of education and later vice-president of the Division of Education and Research of the Ford Foundation: College critics, he claimed, had overlooked "the contribution of advanced education to the personal lives of American citizens and its contributions to their lives as active citizens."[24] Howe based his observations on studies that showed college graduates voted more and participated more in civic affairs than non-college persons.

Nevertheless, it would be unfair to blame educators completely for a situation that was largely the fault of a faltering economy. A bad economy, coupled with an oversupply of college graduates, was mainly to blame for the lessened opportunities for educated youth. Since capitalism requires an oversupply of manpower, it was somewhat ironic that middle-class college graduates found themselves feeling the pinch that traditionally plagued the working class. (In many socialist countries, by contrast, where unemployment is theoretically abolished, the demand for college graduates is high.)

To a certain extent, the declining value of a college degree represented the shifting wage scales of blue- and white-collar employment. That was a result, in large part, of the success of organized labor. Labor has traditionally been blue-collar and has resisted white-collar unionization (AFL-CIO President George Meany never approved of unionizing public schoolteachers, for example), so the weakest and least militant unions have been white-collar unions. It was not surprising that blue-collar, uneducated workers in such roles as sanitationmen, policemen, and firemen in the big cities, along with auto workers and construction workers and teamsters, earned more than the average person with a Ph.D. The fault here lies with the Ph.D. holders who are culturally ill at ease with unions and are too timid and conservative to resort to militant unionization.

Still, the critics of college were excessively pessimistic. Towards the end of the seventies prospects for college graduates were predicted to improve. The Department of Labor forecasted a drop of 3 million college graduates by the 1980s as the World War II baby boom flattened out, thus increasing job opportunities in a less crowded market.[25] By 1976, college graduates had significantly more job offers.[26] Moreover, Herbert Bienstock of the Bureau of Labor Statistics observed that at its worst the recession had affected the non-college graduate the most: In 1975, at the height of the recession, unemployment for college graduates was 2.9 percent compared with 9.1 percent for high school graduates, and 40 percent for black youngsters with or without high school education.[27]

David R. Witmer, assistant chancellor of the University of Wisconsin, challenged Caroline Bird's thesis that college was now a bad investment. His research indicated that the "social return on the college investment has not in fact declined," and although it may do so, this rate of return will still be above that of the 10 percent average rate of return on business investments. Witmer also predicted that there will be a great demand for college graduates within a generation, and that by then, public policy will have come around to the notion that every youngster has a right to college.[28]

Moreover, there had been a dramatic shift in the payoff of college for black and minority students. In the past, studies had shown that for blacks, increased education had not meant increased income due to racial discrimination. The crucial factor accounting for the difference in educational payoffs had been race. For example, Paul Siegal's studies in 1965 and Otis Dudley Duncan's evaluations in 1969 on the weight of education on economic opportunities for blacks concluded that education had little effect in improving the job opportunities of blacks. The main reason for this, the studies stated, was that racial discrimination prevented educated blacks from climbing the economic ladder; Siegal estimated that 40 percent of the difference in black and white incomes resulted from racial discrimination in hiring and promotion.[29] In commenting on these studies, Murray Milner rightly perceived the grist for an educational policy of benign neglect. "These findings could be used to conclude that the attempt to reduce racial inequality through expansion of educational opportunities for Negroes is a relatively poor investment which is likely to yield only small improvements," he observes. "In general, such a conclusion is probably warranted."[30]

Yet, the black rights movement had changed much of the previous aspects of job discrimination. In some cases, that had resulted in preferential hiring for blacks. Indeed, one of the common complaints of militant black groups had been that only the small, educated middle class profited from civil rights struggles to the detriment of the large, lower-class mass of blacks; white liberal organizations sought out promising black college graduates. Milner's studies showed a positive effect of education on occupational opportunities for blacks between 1962 and 1967, precisely during those years that the Civil Rights movement was at its height. By the seventies, the prospects for college-educated blacks had increased even more dramatically. Economist Richard Freeman reported that blacks "have a higher rate of return for investment in college than whites."[31]

For blacks to translate education into higher incomes means the elimination of racism in employment. Certainly, the black rights movement has made appreciable headway. One realls the horror stories of the fifties, perhaps apocryphal, of blacks with Ph.D's forced to work as waiters in railroad restaurants. Today, the contrary is fashionable, for example, showpiece blacks in corporate suites; there has been an upturn recently in black employment in higher paying jobs. Nevertheless, one must be cautious in heedlessly calling for more education without concurrent employment strategies.

As Lester Thurow cautioned a National Manpower Policy Task Force,

> . . . more education will not raise black incomes unless it is combined with complementary training programs, anti-discrimination programs to open job opportunities and equalize payments and good macro-economic programs to insure job availability.[32]

By the seventies, a number of scholars of varied political persuasion took dim views of the efficacy of education. Professor Edward Banfield in *The Unheavenly City* chided "better schooling as 'the solution' to the problems of the city."[33] He questioned the fact that high school graduates earned more than dropouts: It does not necessarily follow, Banfield claimed, that they earned more *"because of anything that they learned in high school."*[34]

But the major study on education and income, which was to influence government policy as well as other academicians, was Christopher Jencks et al.'s *Inequality* published in 1972. Basically, the Jencks study made two main points: (1) that although there is a relationship between educational attainment and income, variations in income can largely be related to personality and factors of chance; (2) that the public schools have no effect on educational mobility, since the most important influence on educational achievement is family background. Jencks concluded that education is not the means for obtaining equality:

> As long as egalitarians assume that public policy cannot contribute to economic equality directly, but must proceed by the ingenious manipulations of marginal institutions like the schools, progress will remain glacial. If we want to move beyond this tradition we will have to establish political control over the economic institutions that shape our society. This is what other countries usually call socialism. Anything less will end in the same disappointment as the reforms of the 1960s.[35]

Jencks argued that only some form of income redistribution would overcome inequality.

Jencks' main evidence was based on a reworking of the Coleman Report of 1966— *Equality of Educational Opportunity*, by James Coleman et al.—which was the second largest social science study, after the Myrdal study on race, in this country. The Coleman study had been commissioned by the Civil Rights Act of 1964 to study integration patterns, but Coleman went beyond that mandate and analyzed school achievement. His conclusion that family background played a decisive role conflicted with evidence in his own study that motivation and self-image among poor blacks proved essential for achievement.

The Jencks thesis was reiterated most notably by Samuel Bowles and Herbert Gintis in *Schooling in Capitalist America*. Gintis had collaborated with Jencks on *Inequality* and later with Bowles developed a strong argument against the relationship between IQ and income. Bowles and Gintis contended that "the educational system serves . . . to reproduce economic inequality and to distort personal development."[36] They concluded that "the creation of an equal and liberating school system requires a revolutionary transformation of economic life."[37]

In a sense, the Jencks-Bowles-Gintis position usefully deflated much of the rhetoric and oversell of educators and politicians, such as President Johnson, who saw in education the answer to all of mankind's social problems. The need to direct energies toward larger social change within the society had been downplayed by the educationists. Jencks' strong critique of education pointed up, once again, the imperative to perceive social problems from a total perspective.

Nevertheless, there are a number of problems with the Jencks study. Whereas Bell exaggerated intellectual merit and underestimated such factors as personality and luck in economic success, Jencks had done the opposite. Jencks verged on reincarnating the Horatio Alger myth in explaining economic advancement in America. Patricia Cayo Sexton showed that income increases with the level of education, and, although one cannot directly attribute a causal relationship, the patterns are so strong they should not be dismissed.[38] There is no dispute that there is a relationship between educational attainment and income. Jencks, however, maintained that, for the most part, educational attainment has been a reflection of the social system, in other words, that few of the poor could take advantage of this system. We know that neither public schools nor colleges educated *large* masses of poor citizens. The work of Colin Greer and Michael Katz, among others, has done much, in this regard, to show how the schools, despite egalitarian rhetoric, actually performed the task of social control. Jencks' study merely confirmed how ineffective our school system has been in this regard, and there is no quarrel with that thrust of his study.

Yet, Jencks underestimated the importance of the credentials society in our economic system. It is one where there is a substantial increase in jobs that demand higher education credentials. Surely, the 40 percent of unemployed black youth in 1977 without college credentials would be better off with some higher education, as statistics showed that the least unemployment was among those with the greatest amount of education.

Nor should one so readily accept Jencks' analysis of the failure of the school reform movement of the sixties and the War on Poverty. Jencks has seriously misread the social dynamics of those initiatives; they did not fail because of inherent flaws in their approach as Jencks maintained, as much as for the political reaction against them. The two attempts to restructure the schools politically—integration and the drive for community control—were countermanded by white parents and school professionals, respectively. The War on Poverty suffered more from a lack of funds, which were redirected to a highly unpopular war in Vietnam, than to the lack of vision of the Great Society.

Moreover, Jencks' (and Coleman's) belief that compensatory education in public schools was inadequate is subject to debate. The scholarly evidence is sufficiently mixed on that score. An important study that preceded Jencks'—James W. Guthrie et al.'s *Schools and Inequality*—argued that schools have had a positive effect on achievement independent of family background. When studies of public-school achievement have been controlled for school effects, rather than family background, the schools have been shown to have positive influence.[39] Moreover, other studies have reported that schools, properly organized, can have some impact. The structured federal Follow Through programs to continue Head Start gains showed considerable achievement gains over conventional classrooms.[40] Sar A. Levitan and Robert Taggart point out that later studies of compensatory education programs initiated by the federal government, such as Head Start, Follow Through, and Title I programs, showed these programs to have a significant influence. They found that "the early national surveys which cast doubt on the impact of compensatory education were premature and far less comprehensive than later state reports."[41] In addition, Professor Benjamin Bloom offered further evidence that the schools can be effective. Bloom's research on experiments in black community colleges led him to conclude that certain methods based on corrective work succeed, so "schools can do an enormous amount to correct for whatever deficiencies children may bring to school."[42]

Jencks makes the same error as Bell in assuming that the educational system provided equality of opportunity, where the best and the brightest could rise. A group of ten black social scientists and educators scored Jencks on that point. They contended that there is a fallacy in Jencks' belief that "schools are, and have been, doing the best they can."[43] That thesis contradicts racism and discrimination in the schools and the historical evidence, most notably the work of Michael Katz, that the public schools tried to keep the poor in their place rather than adapt to the styles of the poor.

Although most of the poor either failed or dropped out of public school in the early twentieth century, some groups— notably the Jews, Chinese, and Greeks—seemed to have flourished in the schools. Although all the evidence is not in, it tends to support the position that educationally minded poor groups took advantage of the public schools and free public colleges in New York City. Historian Diane Ravitch quotes a government report in 1901 that noted that "the city college is practically filled with Jewish pupils . . . [and] . . . in the lower schools, Jewish children are the delight of their teachers for cleverness. . . ."[44] Moreover, three decades later, more than half of New York City's doctors, lawyers, dentists, and public schoolteachers were Jewish. Ravitch concludes that "for the impoverished Jews who crowded into the city's slums in the early twentieth century, the public schools were indeed a ladder 'from the gutter to the university.' "[45] Ravitch's perceptions have been corroborated by other historians such as James W. Sanders, who attested to Jewish precocity in the public schools, and Colin Greer, who found Jewish pupils the least retarded academically of all groups in the immigrant schools.

There were others, however, who challenged the idea that Jewish or any other poor profited through education. Sociologist Herbert Gans, influenced by the Jencks revisionism, flatly concluded that poor Jews did not advance through the schools—an observation that seems to defy both the present and the past. Gans mainly based his evidence on a dissertation by Thomas Kessner later published as *The Golden Door*, studying mobility of Jews at the turn of the century. Kessner's main thesis that Jews progressed rapidly in the work force from blue- to white-collar jobs at the turn of the century has been demonstrated as of little value by a number of researchers who found that individuals commonly went back and forth across these categories with no discernible change in status.[46]

Gans added his own interpretation of why poor Jews did not economically better themselves through education but through labor. Gans is correct in saying that the first Jewish immigrants were not able to take advantage of the schools. However, his belief that poor Jews "were able to escape poverty" because "unskilled labor was in demand at that time" shows little understanding of the economic value of unskilled labor when organized labor was weak, representing less than 3 percent of the work force, and wages were too low and hours too long for anyone to escape anything.[47] Most probably, Jewish merchants and small entrepreneurs fared better. Nevertheless, it seems that a number of Jews—perhaps not the majority—accelerated their climb out of poverty through public schools and a free City University.

What Jencks and his colleagues attempted to accomplish, however, was to *redefine* equality. Whereas both the advocates of meritocracy and the egalitarians invoked the principle of equality of opportunity—the former for those of talent and the latter for everyone—the Jencks theorists argued for equality of *results*. Concluding that education had not, in the past, been effective in social mobility for the large majority of the poor, these new egalitarians believed that only through assuring some measure of equality of outcomes could a just society come about. That equality of results was conceived of in various income-redistribution plans. Many social scientists, serious about meaningful social change, now emphasized the need to redistribute income as the chief means of obtaining equality.

There are political problems with that approach. In a competitive, profit-oriented society such as this one, there is a danger of destroying incentives if income redistribution is sweeping. On the other hand, anything less than substantive income redistribution will fail essentially to change the current social structure. More important, the aim of income redistribution, while laudable, appears politically untenable in this society for some time to come. The national hostility throughout the country among laymen and politicians over the welfare system, for example, gives an indication of the social development of the population. Whereas many are in agreement over some form of equality of opportunity, few seem prepared to accept the concept of equalizing results. Jencks noted also that talk of income redistribution was a "politically irrelevant exercise" given the inclinations of the society.[48] On the other hand, Herbert Gans, a short year later, felt that "income redistribution is an idea whose time has just about arrived."[49] Gans was not especially impressed that Senator George McGovern's presidential campaign in 1972 failed, in part, because of the senator's espousal, for the first time in American presidential politics, of an income-redistribution plan. One social scientist, however, felt that "some people had viewed the 1972 presidential election as a referendum on direct income redistribution."[50] The McGovern proposals were held up to ridicule, and President Nixon was reelected by the biggest vote margin in American history.

Moreover, some socialists, who agreed with the need for income redistribution, were equally concerned that the schools not be dismissed as vehicles to reduce inequality. Patricia Cayo Sexton, for example, argued that the schools are more politically accessible and capable of reform than the entire economic system. In describing the educational failures of the past, Jencks had erroneously prescribed for the future by predicting that better schools would not eliminate poverty. Rather than give up on school reform, Sexton suggested, socialists would be better occupied constructing a new socialist model for our schools that would make them into the first socialist institution in a private society.[51]

Beyond the politics of inequality, there was the more substantive issue of whether equality, certainly for the black poor, could be achieved without attempts to provide both educational opportunity and social change in the economic structure. Some important black scholars were concerned by Jencks' suggestion that blacks need not worry about education. Certainly for blacks, education in the past had not necessarily meant advancement; but with the rise of the black rights struggle in the sixties and the lessening of discrimination through affirmative action policies, blacks with higher education were in demand. Consequently, these scholars felt that Jencks was doing a "disservice to black and low-income children" and providing a coupe de grace to an egalitarian society based on equal educational opportunity.[52]

The danger with the Jencks thesis was that it would reinforce educational conservative policies. That was precisely the tack taken by the Nixon-Ford administrations, neither of which mounted attempts to redistribute income. It was not accidental that Nixon's urban affairs advisor, Daniel P. Moynihan, who was a Harvard colleague of Jencks and whose thinking was similar, should circulate to the presidential cabinet Banfield's polemic, which denied that an urban crisis existed, nor that this same advisor should recommend to the president a policy of "benign neglect" when dealing with insistent black demands for social change.

The Nixon approach, at best, was based on meritocracy. President Nixon had declared that the federal government would see to it that "no *qualified* student who wants to go to college should be barred by lack of money."[53] Vice-President Agnew was much more explicit about condemning universal education based on open admissions and encouraging a meritocracy. On the latter point, the vice-president announced to the press that "certainly, no young man or woman *with ability and talent* should be denied, by the ancient and traditional barriers of poverty, the opportunity to advance to the limits of his capacity" (emphasis added).[54] The Nixon philosophy was consonant with the Banfield and Jencks thrust of not publicly investing large sums in schools and colleges to reduce inequality for the poor. Nixon dismantled many of the Great Society poverty programs and instituted revenue sharing among the states, which removed the focus from federal initiatives. In his State of the Union message in 1970, President Nixon revealed clearly his educational philosophy on equality by excluding education as part of the "range of opportunities for all Americans to fulfill the American dream."[55] Instead, Nixon emphasized voting rights, employment, and ownership as the triad of government priorities to end poverty. In the name of economy, the president pledged that his administration would scuttle "pending programs" even though they may "benefit some of the people" because "their net effect would result in price increases for all the people."[56]

One of these "pending programs" would have attempted to guarantee a college education to all Americans. For some time, the president, Secretary of Health, Education and Welfare Robert Finch, and Commissioner of Education James Allen had such a program before them. This program, first commissioned by President Johnson in the last months of his administration, recommended a system of universal higher education. According to the designers of this program, an unwilling President Nixon had been forced to consider a national universal higher education policy. He had rejected this "pending program"—the legacy of Johnson's Great Society—as too costly.

In October 1968, an amendment to the Higher Education Act of 1965, sponsored by Democratic Senator Ralph Yarborough and Representative James Scheuer, established the groundwork for a national policy on free higher education. Known as the "508 study," it instructed that "on or before December 31, 1969, the President shall submit to Congress proposals relative to the feasibility of making available a post-secondary education to all Americans who qualify and seek it"[57]—in short, a universal higher education law.

Plainly embarrassed by this Democratic maneuver, the incoming Republican president went through the motions of fulfilling the mandate. After a long delay, Office of Education specialists and education consultants from research institutes argued out the semblance of a national higher education policy in a series of small white papers. The Democratic holdovers in the Office of Education, with some outside support, favored a spending program, at least as a long-range goal, whereas Nixon representatives took a more conservative approach. Key issues were the role of the federal government and aid directly to the pupil or to the institution. Following the lead of Clark Kerr's and Harry Rivlin's private studies, most of the papers opted for a spending program that would be institution-oriented with federal cost-of-education supplements. Under the cost-of-education principle, the federal government would reimburse the college for the education of those students who are poor. Although Commissioner Allen favored such a spending program, the White House did not.[58] As a result, the president technically failed to present the recommendation of the 508 study by the required deadline. But for all practical purposes, the 508 study laid buried deep in the presidential desk.

Instead, President Nixon proposed an Educational Opportunity Act, which constituted a mild effort to placate demands that the poor be given a free college education. Mainly, the president amended but one small, current federal program—that of federal loans—so only the poor could now qualify for student loans. By themselves, these student loans acted more as a deterrent than an incentive for college; they were burdensome to repay and only the most ambitious sought them out. It was not surprising that there had been a high rate of default in repaying these loans. In addition, the Nixon administration extended assistance to low-income students in 1972 with Basic Educational Opportunity Grants to the states.

Two major studies on higher education emerged during the Nixon years commissioned by the federal government. The Newman Reports, one issued in 1971 and the other in 1973, presented overviews of American higher education and the changing economic climate. "Our primary intent in the first report was to begin to find ways," Frank Newman, the chairman of the Task Force, explained, "whereby the American approach to higher education could be strengthened by having a more diverse and responsive system, to enlarge the underlying concepts of who can be a student, and when, and what college ought to be all about."[59]

The first report took a non-elitist position and emphasized non-traditional paths to higher education. By the time of the second report, two years later, the Jencks study on education and inequality had been published and it figured strongly in Newman's deliberations. The second report spoke of "the end of guaranteed social mobility" through college—except for blacks and other minorities.[60] Newman conceded that "obviously there is some relationship between a college degree and relatively high status income."[61] But Newman was not sure whether education could be credited for economic advancement—"what is cause and what is effect?"[62]

Newman considered oversupply and underemployment and advocated policy alternatives that were conservative in thrust. Although acknowledging the need for more educational opportunity, Newman concluded that "federal financing for access alone is not enough."[63] What needs to be done is to concentrate federal policy on a "more *effective* system of higher education."[64] Of fifteen points in an agenda for reform, Newman listed help for minorities tenth. That help was not to be in the form of providing greater access at the college level, but, rather, in a two-pronged attack that would establish fellowships at a graduate level (despite the oversupply) and create support for black and other ethnic colleges.

By this time, many private educators questioned the advisability of federal access. The Carnegie Council in 1975 conceded that a national pattern of low or no tuition in two years of college was not possible through "state action alone"; yet achievement of such a pattern "through federal action would be most difficult."[65] Still, the Council concluded that "tuition policy . . . is better subject to state and institutional action, as it has been historically, than to action by the federal government."[66] Instead, the Council recommended that the federal government persist in student assistance as the major federal strategy.

President Ford continued the Nixon educational policies. The Republican party's campaign platform for 1976, for example, emphasized student aid for low-income populations but added that federal higher education policy should also focus on middle-income families as the cost of education soars and that more realistic eligibility guidelines for student aid are essential.

In sum, the crisis in higher education was the result of three main forces: the devolution of mass education into credentialism, a faltering economy, and strategies to reduce inequality based on conservative social science that discounted the mobility of higher education. Only the latter two are susceptible to public policy.

The revamping of a credentials society requires a reform of higher education, to make the college experience and the work experience more compatible. In addition, it requires, equally, reform of the marketplace, where employers are tempted to hire on the basis of academic credentials for non-demanding jobs when there is a large supply of labor. Campus reforms, however, should not eliminate the liberal arts. There are always the happy few for whom college is primarily an intellectual experience rather than simply a career ladder and for whom the world of the intellect is a lifelong pursuit. For most, however, college is primarily an avenue to a decent station in life. It seems more likely that the college is able to adapt than the marketplace.

Bolstering a flagging economy requires national policy incentives on the broadest front. Not least of these would be full employment strategies and some form of income redistribution. The trend for nearly the past fifty years has been for the federal government to assume more responsibility for social policy. Undoubtedly, the cause of the poor has to be advanced on a larger social front as well as by educational strategies to provide equality of opportunity for everyone. In this respect, public policy can greatly influence the educational condition.

NOTES

1. Gail Kennedy, ed., *Education for Democracy* (Boston: D.C. Heath, 1952), p. 26.

2. Ibid., p. 1.

3. Ibid., p. 16.

4. Ibid., p. 8.

5. Ibid.

6. Nelson F. Ashline, Thomas R. Pezzullo, and Charles I. Norris, eds., *Education, Inequality and National Policy* (Lexington, Mass.: Lexington Books, D.C. Heath, 1976), p. xvii.

7. Interview with John Mallan, Urban Institute, Washington, D.C., March 13, 1970 (Phone).

8. Carnegie Commission on Higher Education, *Quality and Equality: New Levels of Federal Responsibility for Higher Education* (New York: Macmillan, 1968).

9. Daniel Bell, *The Coming of Post-Industrial Society* (New York: Basic Books, 1973), p. 129.

10. Ibid., pp. 215-16.

11. Christopher Jencks and David Riesman, *The Academic Revolution* (Garden City, N.Y.: Doubleday, 1968), pp. 99-100.

12. Ibid., p. 153.

13. *Parade*, August 8, 1976, p. 16.

14. James O'Toole, "The Reserve Army of the Underemployed," *Change*, May 1975, p. 28.

15. Ibid.

16. Ivar Berg, "Rich Man's Qualifications for Poor Man's Jobs," *Transaction*, March 1969, p. 50.

17. Ibid.

18. Ibid.

19. Samuel Bowles and Herbert Gintis, *Schooling in Capitalist America* (New York: Basic Books, 1976), p. 28.

20. *Newsweek*, April 23, 1966, p. 61.

21. Ibid.

22. Caroline Bird, *The Case Against College* (New York: Bantam, 1975), p. 62.

23. Richard B. Freeman, *The Overeducated American* (New York: Academic Press, 1976), pp. 117-36.

24. Harold Howe II, *The Value of College: A Non-Economist's View* (New York: Ford Foundation Report, 1975).

25. *Chronicle of Higher Education*, May 10, 1976, p. 6.

26. *Long Island Press*, August 16, 1966, p. 11.

27. *New York Times*, May 16, 1966, Sect. 11, p. 12.

28. David R. Witmer, "Is the Value of College Going Really Declining?" *Change*, December 1976, p. 60.

29. Murray Milner, *Effects of Federal Aid to Higher Education on Social and Educational Inequality* (New York: Center for Policy Research, 1970), p. 127.

30. Ibid.

31. Freeman, *The Overeducated American*, p. 144.

32. Lester Thurow, "Redistribution Aspects of Manpower Training Program" (Washington: 1971), p. 7.

33. Edward Banfield, *The Unheavenly City* (Boston: Little, Brown, 1970), p. 134.

34. Ibid.

35. Christopher Jencks et al., *Inequality* (New York: Basic Books, 1972), p. 265.

36. Bowles and Gintis, *Schooling in Capitalist America*, p. 48.

37. Ibid., p. 265.

38. Patricia Cayo Sexton, *Education and Income* (New York: Viking Press, 1961).

39. Patricia Cayo Sexton, "The Inequality Affair: A Critique of Jencks," *Social Policy*, September-October 1973, p. 59.

40. Marshall S. Smith, "Equal Opportunity—Some Promise and a Lack of Vision," in Ashline, Pezzullo, and Norris, eds., *Education, Inequality, and National Policy*, p. 181.

41. Sar A. Levitan and Robert Taggart, *The Promise of Greatness* (Cambridge: Harvard University Press, 1976), p. 128.

42. *New York Times*, June 9, 1976, p. 43.

43. Ronald Edmonds et al., "A Black Response to Christopher Jencks' *Inequality* and Certain Other Issues," *Harvard Educational Review* 43, no. 1 (February 1973): 82.

44. Diane Ravitch, *The Great School Wars* (New York: Basic Books, 1974), p. 178.

45. Ibid.

46. Richard W. Fox, Review of *The Golden Door*, by Thomas Kessner, *Chronicle of Higher Education*, May 23, 1977, p. 12.

47. Herbert Gans, "The Role of Education in the Escape from Poverty," in Ashline, Pezzullo, and Norris, eds., *Education, Inequality, and National Policy*, p. 65.

48. Jencks, *Inequality*, p. 263.

49. Herbert Gans, *More Equality* (New York: Pantheon, 1973), p. 149.

50. Lester C. Thurow, "Problems Without Solutions: Solutions Without Problems," in Ashline, Pezzullo, and Norris, eds., *Education, Inequality, and National Policy*, p. 165.

51. Sexton, "The Inequality Affair," pp. 53-71.

52. Edmonds et al., "A Black Response," p. 79.

53. Spiro T. Agnew, "Toward a 'Middle Way' in College Admissions," *Educational Record*, Spring 1970, p. 109.

54. Ibid.

55. *New York Times*, January 23, 1970, p. 22.

56. Ibid.

57. Public Law 90-575, 90th Cong., S.3769, Amend. 1968. Higher Education Act of 1965.

58. Interview with John Mallan, Urban Institute, Washington, D.C., March 13, 1970 (Phone).

59. Frank Newman, "A Preview of the Second Newman Report," *Change*, May 1972, p. 36.

60. Frank Newman et al., *The Second Newman Report: National Policy and Higher Education* (Cambridge: MIT Press, 1974), p. 19.

61. Ibid.

62. Ibid.

63. Ibid., p. 80.

64. Ibid.

65. Carnegie Council on Policy Studies in Higher Education, *Low or No Tuition* (San Francisco: Jossey-Bass, 1975), p. 2.

66. Ibid.

CHAPTER 7

A scenario for the future: the urban-grant university

The social movement of the 1960s propelled the urban university into the forefront of educational reform. However, efforts by urban university administrators—spurred by student and community protest—to involve the university in the affairs of the city diminished by the 1970s. An economic recession, a public reaction to the excesses of student radicals, a new quiet on the campuses and in the ghettoes, and, most important, a conservative national policy—all these developments blunted the drive for a full realization of the urban university. Historian Michael Katz in *Class, Bureaucracy and Schools* discovered that educational reform in America has always been a by-product of a larger social movement. Perhaps one must await another large-scale social movement before the urban university will fully come into its own.

First, however, the national hostility to the city, most recently reflected in the 1975 New York City fiscal crisis, must be overcome. The agrarian myth has adversely influenced the development of the urban university. Even the most progressive proposal to create an urban university system emerged from the thought grooves of the agrarian land-grant movement. In 1958, Paul Ysvilaker of the Ford Foundation, at the 44th Biennial Meeting of the Association of Urban Universities, first proposed a system of urban-grant universities. What the federal government should do, he argued, is create a system of federal urban-grant universities similar to that created by the Morrill Act for agriculture.[1] These urban-grant universities would be the pertinent universities the cities needed, emphasizing urban studies. To show the federal government the way, the Ford Foundation, under Ysvilaker's prodding, created a num-

125

ber of urban centers at specified universities. (It was not accidental that the first director of Rutgers urban-studies program had gained a national reputation as an agrarian scholar at a land-grant school.)

Ysvilaker's idea was seconded six years later by President Johnson.[2] Clark Kerr, with further thoughts on his concept of the multiversity, proposed a system of sixty-seven urban-grant universities, federally funded, nearly a decade after Ysvilaker's original suggestion. Kerr argued that these urban-grant universities be in cities with a minimum of 250,000 people, and that they should work on the problems of the city through experiment stations much as the land-grant colleges had worked on the problems of the land. Moreover, Kerr suggested that this aid should come directly from the federal government, rather than from the federal to the state government and then to the urban-grant university.[3]

One reason there has been no overall national policy for urban universities has been the lack of lobbying activity by concerned university administrators and their clientele.[4] In spring 1976, however, twenty urban public universities from California to New York formed the Committee of Urban Public Universities to lobby for a federal program of urban-grant universities. The committee later changed part of its focus and its name to Committee for Urban Program Universities after it was thought to be more politically advantageous to broaden its membership to include urban private universities as well. The committee employed a full-time lobbyist in Washington whose major responsibility was to educate and lobby congress for an urban-grant university program.

The committee's aims were rather modest. They defined an urban-grant university for their purposes as one located in a major city with over 500,000 population (twice Kerr's model), with a substantial portion of its students from the cities, and one that had been involved in urban affairs. They sought to obtain an Urban Grant University Act of 1977 that would authorize some $25 million the first year with subsequent appropriate funding for the next five years. These monies would encourage urban research and urban extension-type projects. According to the committee, those urban universities with high institutional quality and competence in urban affairs should be designated urban-grant universities. By June 1977, fifty-three members of the House of Representatives, mostly from industrial and urbanized states, joined in sponsoring the Urban Grant University Act (H.R. 7328, 95th Congress). Although the committee's lobbyist was optimistic over this thrust by the large urban universities for an urban-grant university program, he estimated, nevertheless, that the passage of such a program was, at best, some years away.[5]

The urban-grant concept had failed, in the past, to enlist a large and powerful constituency in its behalf. Perhaps that was due to the agrarian overtones of the urban-grant proposal. The land-grant movement was bound up with the concrete realities of an agrarian national economy. The urban-grant movement, on the other hand, appeared nebulous and not tied to a national economic program.

One problem seemed to be that urban research and agricultural research were quite different. Some critics felt it was one thing for a land-grant school to supply a farmer with research that would improve the quality of his fertilizer. It was quite another thing, they felt, for an urban university to supply research to improve the conditions of the city. The Ford Foundation, in reviewing their urban extension programs, concluded that:

Urban research, on the other hand, tends to be conceptual, explanatory, and exhortatory. There are no direct benefits to Negro families, groping mayors, and harrassed health and welfare councils from even a first-rate research monograph on the history of building permits or the prevision of the future metropolis. Agricultural extension was a useful device for helping further the education of men and women who lived in areas too remote or thinly settled for adequate facilities. But the stubborn educational problems of the city are usually due not to a lack of nearby schools but to a lack of motivation, cultural barriers, defects in the school, or all of these. The student of urbanism can describe, classify, or theorize about such shortcomings, but ideas for direct solution come hard and slowly.[6]

Granted the complexities of urban problems, one still asks why urban research cannot still perform a function similar to that of the land-grant colleges. Surely, using the educational analogy of the Ford Foundation writer, urban research that is policy-oriented can bring about an improvement in the educational achievement of city school youngsters. Studies are showing, for example, that class size

has an effect on school achievement. It would appear logical, therefore, for educational policy makers to seek to reduce the sizes of
urban classrooms. In short, one can expect tangible results from
policy-oriented urban research.

Still, on a national front, the urban-grant university does not
have clear economic or political implications. Of what practical
benefit is an urban-grant university, federal legislators ask? Congress has only moved into the educational arena when it felt its
national economic interest was at stake: The Land Ordinance of
1785, for example, insured the orderly settlement of the northwest
by stipulating that 1.16 of each township would be marked for free
public schools; the Morrill Act promoted agriculture; the GI Bill
of Rights and the National Defense Act of 1958 insured a corps of
trained scientific manpower for Cold War purposes. The urban-
grant proposal merely borrowed the trappings of the Morrill Act
without the substance.

Yet, the urban-grant idea is not without merit. It seems more
plausible at present than when Ysvilaker suggested it twenty years
ago. What has given it new meaning is the need to develop urban
universities that will meet the new responsibilities of educating an
urban poor and constructing a science of urbanology to solve the
growing and enormous problems of the cities. When Ysvilaker introduced his scheme, large-scale poverty had not been "officially"
rediscovered (that came four years later with the publication of
Michael Harrington's *The Other America* and the subsequent federal War on Poverty program) in all its complexity and with its
large urban base. Moreover, our urban colleges and universities
had not been beseiged by students to reform themselves to become
"relevant," that is, to address themselves both in form and substance to the social problems of the cities.

The proponents of urban-grant universities have suggested the
creation of twenty to seventy colleges by the federal government in
cities throughout the country, although never fully defining any
special character or purpose for them. It seems evident that this
concept of the federal urban college system is realistic and appropriate. Cities do not have sufficient resources to make these institutions effective and state governments are already committed to
their own university systems. Their interest in urban areas has been

historically deficient. A federal college system comprised of highly autonomous colleges in cities throughout the country is long overdue. Spread through fifty cities of large- and middle-sized populations, these institutions would provide a new and much needed national resource. Much of the benefit would accrue to the national agencies engaged in urban affairs and to the development of national policy in these areas. Federal grants for research in these areas have already been enormous and were necessarily spread across the country to institutions that had no special competence in this area and that rarely related to each other.

The prospects of an urban-grant university program are linked with the larger question of the amount of federal aid to higher education. Enlightened educators, especially in the Carnegie Foundation, have argued for the past decade for a progressive increase in federal aid as the only solution to the problems of higher education. They had hoped that Washington would double its investment by the mid-seventies to account for one-half the total costs of higher education, and that by the end of the century, the federal government would be paying all of the bills. Unfortunately, the percentage of federal aid to higher education did not substantially increase.

The Carnegie Foundation issued a series of reports on higher education during the past decade. These reports distilled the conventional wisdom of educators concerning the federal role. The 1968 report proceeded from the premise that the major financing of higher education must be shifted from state and local governments and private sources to the federal government *gradually*. Whereas 75 to 80 percent of our higher education costs were not paid with federal funds, the economic reality was such that by the commission's immediate target date of 1976, nearly one-third of these educational funds would come from Washington.[7] To accomplish this aim, the report merely extended concepts already instituted by other federal acts, such as the GI Bill and the Higher Education Act of 1965. What the Carnegie report sought was a mild enlargement of the federal role—sufficient to establish the federal principle—within a feasible deadline. The report revealed no new departures or radical notions. Rather, it was a considered statement of short-range goals that would increase the educational opportunities somewhat.

By 1975, Carnegie recommended that federal support for higher education should be 50 percent.[8] Carnegie estimated that the bill for all higher education would be in the vicinity of $11.5 billion. The major value of the Carnegie studies in this area has been that they were eminently practical and in certain instances influenced national policy. The studies gave official approval to the trend towards federalization. But they did so in educational, political, and economic terms that could be accomplished without undue strain on the national budget or to the political balance of power.

National policy towards urban universities must, in time, go beyond the limits of urban research and urban extension and deal with two other key issues: university expansion into surrounding neighborhoods, and the provison for greater access to the urban poor.

One solution for the problems of university expansion in the city would be for the federal government to institute a "good-neighbor" policy. Instead of providing tax and other financial inducements such as those under Section 112 of the Urban Renewal Act for university expansion, Washington could legislate financial benefits to universities that build decent low-income housing for its poor communities. For the university, this good-neighbor policy could mean a sound business as well as a social investment. Part of this low-income housing could be used for students and faculty. For Washington, this policy could supplement many model-cities types of low-income projects.

Most important, national policy for urban-grant universities should be framed in terms of realizing the goal of universal access to higher education. This would entail policies for urban-grant universities of free tuition and open admissions. The concept of free tuition is an integral part of a society's total concept of higher education. A commitment to universal mass higher education, and particularly urban higher education, would automatically require a commitment to free tuition, as was true in primary and secondary education. The only limitation would then be in terms of the priorities of the society in the distribution of public funds. The price of higher education is a powerful deterrent against college for the urban poor.

Free tuition is a concept that has enlisted widespread verbal support but has never really been accepted as a workable arrangement in higher education in America. Undoubtedly, the concept is tied up with the principle of selective higher education. Needless to say, those who could afford tuition have always been categorized as part of the especially qualified group. For those who *are qualified* but who cannot afford to pay their way, there is a long tradition of "charity" or "scholarship" to ease their task. This has assumed, however, an awareness of the existence of such aids and a high degree of competence on the part of the candidate to compete for support. The private college or university long ago established the monetary standards for higher education in America. Free tuition at wholly public institutions might have constituted a serious threat (or at least they perceived it as a threat) to the private institutions and they proved, particularly in the east, to be a constant force opposing such a movement. Tuition was also tied to the Protestant ethic: those who worked hard enough, the fittest, would find a way to manage the costs. To them would go the rewards of higher education; what better way to separate the chaff from the wheat?

The longest tradition for free tuition rested in the City University of New York. The history of that policy, the purpose and philosophy of these institutions, is noteworthy. These colleges, each separately established over a period of eighty years throughout New York City, were intended to service the city population (none of the colleges, for example, provided for residence on the campus), a population that could not afford the costs of tuition and board at colleges away from home.

The end of free tuition in New York's City University in 1976 was not lost on black and Puerto Rican political figures. Percy Sutton, the black Manhattan Borough president, and Herman Badillo, the Puerto Rican congressman, made strong statements in favor of free tuition in the 1977 Democratic primary contest for mayor of the city of New York. Badillo, a poor boy who would not have gone to college without the "free ticket" of City College, characterized the ending of free tuition as a "stupid decision" that was "cruel" because it "sells out the future of so many young people," and that "unless free tuition is restored, New York is going to become a city of endless poverty."[9]

Even with a policy of free tuition, the urban poor could not fully take advantage of the system in the past; they disqualified them-

selves (or were disqualified) early in their lives by dropping out of
school to get gainful employment. Their lack of knowledge of the
system was also a factor, although there is no way to measure the
extent of this problem. The night college established in the city colleges was an attempt to service a group of students who were forced
to hold full-time jobs. Adjustments were made (against faculty pressure) in standards to suit better the needs of that clientele. After a
time, the evening schools became a track for entry into the day colleges for those students unable to meet the requirements.

Realistically, free tuition in itself cannot fulfill concepts of mass
higher education; it can only ease the way for those who are already
upwardly mobile. To reach the lowest economic levels, payment to
students for support would be a necessary arrangement. Also, access to adequate lower and secondary school preparation and ex-
posure to what college offers are necessary prerequisites to a system
committed to mass higher education.

Incentives for higher education may well vary. There are those
sons and daughters of union members in "grandfather-clause"
unions who may see little advantage in a college education. In every
society the incentives must be adjusted to other institutional development. What would seem appropriate in a purportedly egalitarian
society would be access to higher education both in terms of awareness and preparation and also financial competence. For any plan
for mass education to be accepted, the diversity in institutions would
have to be greatly encouraged and expanded.

The diversification of urban higher education would preserve the
sanctuaries of those who can afford to pay in the private institutions
but it would also require the expansion of wholly urban public institutions for the largest segment of the population. There is a serious problem, even a conflict, for those who seek to maintain the
diversity of institutions. The private college or university has depended on public support in different forms throughout its history.
Early in their history, colleges received direct aid from state governments. After the creation of the state university system aid took
the form of special program funds, such as the agriculture school
at Cornell, scholarship money for state students, and finally research
support. Later, this included extensive federal funding for research
and more recently for construction funds. MIT received 80 percent

of its funds from the federal government; yet, it would designate itself as a private institution, not subject to any fulfillment of public policy or constraints in admission.[10]

The Bundy Plan for higher education in New York State embodied the concept of maintaining diversity through public support of private institutions.[11] Even avoiding the church-state question (which involves federal and state support of parochial or religious institutions), one must be concerned with the degree to which the use of public funds for these purposes limits the fulfillment of its role by the public institution. Public funds are not limitless and choices are necessary. When arrangements for influencing the admissions policies and service roles of the private institutions are suggested, the reactions are strong and loud. Yet, the allocations of public monies for these purposes requires some form of control. It should not be unthinkable, for example, that a certain percentage of quota admissions by lottery to urban private institutions be a requirement for granting of public funds.

One of the other major conflicts developing over a universal open-admissions policy in higher education (universal, meaning with high-school credentials, which is, in itself, restrictive) is the selective proces of placement. The mushrooming of the two-year junior or community college is not without purpose. It has become the college for the "poorer" student, whether by academic or income standards. The middle-class student with access to a more college-oriented secondary-school education is more likely to meet the requirements of the high-status four-year institution. There is serious question that all of the standardized tests and other measurements for selective admissions do any more than reflect that difference in preparation. Also, experimental programs with the "nonqualified" have proven that once in college (even at the most elite institutions), these people fare very well. This would suggest a value in at least experimenting with a lottery system of distribution of students in public colleges, particularly in those institutions that claim to support open admissions.

Long-range resolution of this conflict would be more readily attainable if the diversification of higher education were greatly expanded and the special areas of competence of individual students were fully recognized and their development encouraged by the primary and secondary schools. Some stratification geared to the status system of the society will always prevail (unless there is a complete leveling of the economic system), but with diversification and closer attention to individual competence its impact on the individual or group of students would be minimized. Certainly, the human-resource development under such an approach would be a great boon to American society.

The alternatives to reducing inequality in education are few. A quota system, although politically improbable, presents one method. It must be remembered, the quarrel at City College initially centered on quotas. All protagonists accepted the proposition that admissions could not be truly universal, and they proposed different versions of quota plans. The first demand of the black students was for quotas.

One consideration might be preferentially to admit blacks and Puerto Ricans and other minorities to private and public colleges to immediately reduce income gaps as was done with the GI Bill of Rights. By creating a supply of more black college graduates and by reducing the number of white college graduates, the impact on the economy might decrease racial income differentials. This quota system would narrow the income gap. Therefore, politically unpalatable but economically desirable would be a plan to reduce the number of white college admissions at the same time that the number of black college admissions was increased. Since American college administrators have *always* pursued some form of quota and random selection—whether by admitting a token number of rich and poor, or a token number of students from various geographical areas—they would not be possessed of the "strange madness," as Vice-President Spiro Agnew claimed, were they to choose students on the basis of a minority quota system. Bowdoin College, in Brunswick, Maine, has dropped traditional admissions policies to permit just that. Bowdoin's lead should be followed by other private colleges but has yet to be. What they have done, of course, is merely adjust a prevalent policy of quotas and random selections to favor a black poor.

Other ways to speed up the education of a black and minority urban poor would be to create entirely new forms of education. These might consist of experimental colleges geared to existing high-paying jobs and not bound by traditional credentialing involved in our present undergraduate schools. They could be small, decentralized units constituting an ambulatory higher education component serving a wide area. Already there are notable examples of this nature, such as the University Without Walls, which stresses self-directed study and takes into account life experience.

Some control over admissions of publicly funded private universities would be necessary. This is extremely important in light of the pressure by private universities to obtain direct state and federal support. The reaction of private universities to a national policy of open admissions, of course, may be to tighten their admissions policies despite their heavy subsidization. That is, the private universities may well create a two-tracked system of unequal education, while receiving large amounts of public aid. Therefore, it would be incumbent for the dispensing government to place limits on that aid. Private universities would have to liberalize their admissions requirements to admit the poor free, on a quota basis, if they are to receive public support. One wishes the largest amount of educational options, rather than a complete public system of education. However, for a private university to receive public financing and yet discriminate against a needy public would be intolerable.

Yet, for higher education to attempt single-handedly to redress social inequities would be foolhardy. The university must assume that there will be in the society large-scale reform in employment and the decrease of racism. On the other hand, for the university to accept the notion that no such reforms are forthcoming, and thus not to act, would be unconscionable. One area in which the university could exercise leadership would be in public schooling. Urban-grant universities might have to venture boldly into ghetto education. That would probably mean adopting schools and working innovatively towards their improvement. A handful of such experiments exist where enterprising professors took a lead; however, these new relationships would have to be institutional and not merely the result of the initiative of some far-seeing faculty.

But it is doubtful whether efforts to provide for open, free, committed urban colleges will be successful without strong federal leadership and support. Consequently, the creation of the federal urban-grant university appears to be the best means of realizing the potential of the urban university to meet the diverse needs of a nation of cities.

NOTES

1. J. Martin Klotscke, *The Urban University and the Future of Our Cities* (New York: Harper & Row, 1969), p. 51.

2. Kenneth J. Vandevelde and Jessie L. Miller, "The Urban Grant University Concept: A Systems Analysis," *Behavioral Science* 20, no. 5 (September 1975): 274.

3. Clark Kerr, *The Urban-Grant University: A Model for the Future*, No. 8 of the City College Papers (New York: City College, 1968), pp. 6-8.

4. Thomas P. Murphy and Elizabeth Knipe, "The Federal Government and Urban Higher Education," in *Universities in the Urban Crisis*, ed. Thomas P. Murphy (New York: Dunellen, 1974), p. 353.

5. Interview with Jim Harrison, Executive Director, Committee of Urban Program Universities, Washington, D.C., June 20, 1977 (Phone).

6. Ford Foundation, *Urban Extension* (New York: 1966), pp. 6-7.

7. Carnegie Commission on Higher Education, *Quality and Equality: New Levels of Federal Responsibility for Higher Education* (New York: Macmillan, 1968).

8. Carnegie Council on Policy Studies in Higher Education, *The Federal Role in Post-Secondary Education: Unfinished Business 1975-1980* (San Francisco: Jossey-Bass, 1975).

9. *Village Voice*, June 27, 1977, p. 26.

10. James Ridgeway, *The Closed Corporation* (New York: Random House, 1968), p. 5.

11. Report of the Select Committee on the Future of Private and Independent Higher Education, *New York State and Private Higher Education* (New York: 1968).

Bibliography

BOOKS

Allmendinger, David F., Jr. *Paupers and Scholars*. New York: St. Martin's Press, 1975.

Ashline, Nelson F.; Pezzullo, Thomas R.; and Norris, Charles I., eds. *Education, Inequality and National Policy*. Lexington, Mass.: Lexington Books, D.C. Heath, 1976.

Banfield, Edward. *The Unheavenly City*. Boston: Little, Brown, 1970.

Barzun, Jacques. *The American University*. New York: Harper & Row, 1968.

Bell, Daniel. *The Coming of Post-Industrial Society*. New York: Basic Books, 1973.

Berg, Ivar. *Education and Jobs: The Great Training Robbery*. New York: Praeger, 1970.

Bird, Caroline. *The Case Against College*. New York: Bantam, 1975.

Bowles, Samuel, and Gintis, Herbert. *Schooling in Capitalist America*. New York: Basic Books, 1976.

Boyle, Kay. *The Long Walk at San Francisco State*. New York: Grove Press, 1970.

Carnegie Commission on Higher Education. *Quality and Equality: New Levels of Federal Responsibility for Higher Education*. New York: Macmillan, 1968.

Carnegie Council on Policy Studies in Higher Education. *The Campus and the City*. New York: McGraw-Hill, 1972.

――――. *Low or No Tuition*. San Francisco: Jossey-Bass, 1975.

――――. *The Federal Role in Post-secondary Education: Unfinished Business, 1975-1980*. San Francisco: Jossey-Bass, 1975.

137

Coleman, James S., et al. *Equality of Educational Opportunity*. Washington, D.C.: U.S. Government Printing Office, 1966.

Cox Commission. *Crisis at Columbia*. New York: Vintage, 1968.

Eddy, Jr., Edward Danforth. *Colleges for Our Land and Time: The Land-Grant Idea in American Education*. New York: Harper & Brothers, 1957.

Eldredge, H. Wentworth, ed. *Taming Megalopolis*. Vol. II. New York: Anchor, 1967.

Fiedler, Leslie. *Love and Death in the American Novel*. New York: World, 1962.

Ford, Nick Aaron. *Black Studies*. Port Washington, N.Y.: Kennikat Press, 1973.

Franklin, Raymond S., and Resnick, Solomon. *The Political Economy of Racism*. New York: Holt, Rhinehart & Winston, 1973.

Freeman, Richard B. *The Overeducated American*. New York: Academic Press, 1976.

Galbraith, John Kenneth. *The New Industrial State*. Boston: Houghton Mifflin, 1967.

Gans, Herbert. *More Equality*. New York: Pantheon, 1973.

Glazer, Nathan, and Moynihan, Daniel Patrick. *Beyond the Melting Pot*. Cambridge, Mass.: The MIT Press, 1963.

Gordon, David M., ed. *Problems in Political Economy: An Urban Perspective*. 2nd ed. Lexington, Mass: D.C. Heath, 1977.

Grant, Joanne. *Confrontation on Campus*. New York: Signet, 1969.

Greeley, Andrew M., and Rossi, Peter H. *The Education of Catholic Americans*. Chicago: Aldine, 1966.

Greer, Colin. *The Great School Legend*. New York: Basic Books, 1972.

Guthrie, James W., et al. *Schools and Inequality*. Cambridge: MIT Press, 1971.

Gutman, Herbert G. *The Black Family in Slavery and Freedom, 1750-1925*. New York: Pantheon, 1977.

Haley, Alex. *Roots*. New York: Doubleday, 1976.

Handlin, Oscar, and Burchard, John, eds. *The Historian and the City*. Cambridge: MIT Press, 1963.

Harrington, Michael. *The Other America*. New York: Macmillan, 1962.

Jencks, Christopher, et al. *Inequality*. New York: Basic Books, 1972.

Jencks, Christopher, and Riesman, David. *The Academic Revolution*. Garden City, N.Y.: Doubleday, 1968.

Katz, Irwin, ed. *Race and the Social Sciences*. New York: Basic Books, 1969.

Katz, Michael B. *Class, Bureaucracy and Schools.* New York: Praeger, 1971.
————. *The Irony of Early School Reform.* Cambridge: Harvard University Press, 1968.
Kennedy, Gail, ed. *Education for Democracy.* Lexington, Mass.: D.C. Heath, 1952.
Kerr, Clark. *The Uses of the University.* New York: Harper & Row, 1966.
Klotscke, J. Martin. *The Urban University and the Future of Our Cities.* New York: Harper & Row, 1966.
Kolbe, Parke. *Urban Influences in Higher Education in England and the United States.* New York: Macmillan, 1928.
Levitan, Sar A., and Taggart, Robert. *The Promise of Greatness.* Cambridge: Harvard University Press, 1976.
Liebow, Eliot. *Tally's Corner.* Boston: Little, Brown, 1967.
Loewenstein, Louis K., *Urban Studies.* New York: Free Press, 1977.
Murphy, Thomas P., ed. *Universities in the Urban Crisis.* New York: Dunellen, 1975.
Nash, George. *The University and the City: Eight Cases of Involvement.* New York: McGraw-Hill, 1973.
Newman, Frank, et al. *Report on Higher Education.* Washington: U.S. Government Printing Office, 1971.
————. *The Second Newman Report: National Policy and Higher Education.* Cambridge: MIT Press, 1974.
Olson, Keith W. *The G.I. Bill, the Veterans, and the Colleges.* Lexington, Ky.: The University Press of Kentucky, 1974.
Ravitch, Diane. *The Great School Wars.* New York: Basic Books, 1974.
Reynolds, Ora E. *The Social and Economic Status of College Students.* New York: Teachers College Press, 1927.
Ridgeway, James. *The Closed Corporation.* New York: Random House, 1968.
Robinson, Armstead L., et al. *Black Studies in the University.* New Haven: Yale University Press, 1969.
Rosen, David; Brunner, Seth; and Fowler, Steve. *Open Admissions: The Promise & the Lie of Open Access to American Higher Education.* Lincoln, Neb.: University of Nebraska Press, 1973.
Rudolph, Frederic. *The American College and University.* New York: Knopf, 1962.
Rudy, S. Willis. *The College of the City of New York: A History 1847-1947.* New York: The City College Press, 1949.

Ryan, William. *Blaming the Victim.* New York: Pantheon, 1971.
Sanders, James W. *The Education of an Urban Minority.* New York: Oxford University Press, 1976.
Sexton, Patricia Cayo. *Education and Income.* New York: Viking Press, 1961.
Wagner, Geoffrey. *The End of Education.* New York: A.S. Barnes, 1976.
Who's Who in America 1970. Chicago: A.N. Marquis, 1970.
Willingham, Warren. *Free-Access Higher Education.* Princeton: College Entrance Examination Board, 1970.
Worthy, William. *The Rape of Our Neighborhoods.* New York: Wm. Morrow, 1976.
Young, Michael. *The Rise of the Meritocracy.* Middlesex, Eng.: Penguin, 1961.

REPORTS AND UNPUBLISHED MATERIAL

Carroll, Robert L., et al. *University-Community Tension and Urban Campus Form.* Cincinnati: University of Cincinnati, October 1972.
Columbia University. *The Human Uses of the University.* New York: 1969.
Conference of Urban Study Center Directors. "University Urban Studies Centers—Observations from Within." Detroit, Mich.: Wayne State University, March 27-29, 1969.
Council of University Institutes for Urban Affairs. *Proceedings of the First Annual Conference.* Washington: 1970.
———. *Urban Affairs in Transition.* Atlanta: 1976.
Education USA Special Report. *Black Studies in Schools.* Washington: 1969.
Ford Foundation. *Urban Extension.* New York: 1966.
Howe II, Harold. *The Value of College: A Non-Economist's View.* New York: Ford Foundation Report, 1975.
Kerr, Clark. *The Urban-Grant University: A Model for the Future.* No. 8 of the City College Papers. New York: City College, 1968.
Levine, Susan. "Open Admissions at Queens College." New York: 1971.
Love, Theresa R. *Possible Directions for Black Studies in American Colleges & Universities.* St. Louis, Mo.: ERIC Document Reproduction Service, ED 103-869, 1974.
Milner, Murray. *Effects of Federal Aid to Higher Education on Social and Educational Inequality.* New York: Center for Policy Research, 1970.

National Center for Educational Statistics. *The Condition of Education.* Washington: U.S. Government Printing Office, 1976.

Pendelton, William C. *Urban Studies and the University: The Ford Foundation Experience.* New York: Ford Foundation, April 1974.

Queens College Report. Fall 1969.

Report of the Select Committee on the Future of Private and Independent Higher Education. *New York State and Private Higher Education.* New York: 1968.

Slayton, William. *The University, The City and Urban Renewal.* Washington: American Council on Education, 1963.

Smith, William Deane. "Wayne State and Its Neighbors." Detroit: Center for Urban Studies, Wayne State University, 1969.

Thurow, Lester. "Redistribution Aspects of Manpower Training Programs." Washington: 1971.

Urban Research Corporation. *Guns on Campus: Student Protest at Cornell.* Chicago: 1970.

———. *Harvard's Student Strike: The Politics of Mass Mobilization.* Chicago: 1970.

———. *Student Protests 1969.* Chicago: 1970.

ARTICLES

Agnew, Spiro T. "Toward a 'Middle Way' in College Admissions." *Educational Record*, Spring 1970.

Berg, Ivar. "Rich Man's Qualifications for Poor Man's Jobs." *Transaction*, March 1969.

Billings, Thomas. "Black Education and White Liberalism." *New Leader*, December 22, 1969.

Brozan, Nadine. "Life on a Treadmill: Financing College for Several Children." *New York Times*, October 21, 1976.

Cass, James. "Can the University Survive the Black Challenge." *Saturday Review*, June 21, 1969.

Clark, Kenneth. "Black Studies: The Antioch Case." *The Antioch Review*, Summer 1969.

Cleaver, Eldridge. "Education and Revolution." *The Black Scholar* 1, no. 1 (November 1969).

Collins, Randall. "Some Comparative Principles of Educational Stratification." *Harvard Educational Review* 47, no. 1 (February 1977).

Edmonds, Ronald, et al. "A Black Response to Christopher Jencks' *Inequality* and Certain Other Issues." *Harvard Educational Review* 43, no. 1 (February 1973).

Epstein, Jason. "The Last Days of New York." *New York Review of Books*, February 19, 1976.

Friesema, H. Paul. "Urban Studies and Action Research." *Urban Affairs Quarterly* 7, no. 1 (September 1971).

Genovese, Eugene. "Black Studies: Trouble Ahead." *The Atlantic*, June 1969.

Greeley, Andrew M. "The New Urban Studies—A Word of Caution." *Educational Record*, Summer 1970.

Harrington, Michael. "Keep Open Admissions Open." *New York Times Magazine*, November 2, 1975.

Healy, Timothy S. "Will Everyman Destroy the University?" *Saturday Review*, December 20, 1969.

Huber, James H. "Urban Studies: An Opportunity for Synthesis Among Social Policy Sciences." *Intellect* 104, no. 2369 (November 1975).

Jaffe, A.J., and Adams, Walter. "Open Admissions and Academic Quality." *Change*, March-April 1971, p. 11.

Jenkins, Martin D., and Reis, Bernard H. "The Urban Involvement of Higher Education: An Analysis of Selected Trends and Issues." *Journal of Higher Education* XVII, no. 4 (July-August 1975): 401.

Karabel, Jerome. "Perspectives on Open Admissions." *Educational Record* 53, no. 1 (Winter 1972).

Kristol, Irving, and Weaver, Paul. "Who Knows New York? Notes on a Mixed-up City." *The Public Interest*, no. 16 (Summer 1969).

Lythcott, Stephen. "Black Studies: The Antioch Case." *The Antioch Review* (Summer 1969).

Newman, Frank. "A Preview of the Second Newman Report." *Change*, May 1972.

O'Toole, James. "The Reserve Army of the Underemployed." *Change*, May 1975, p. 28.

Popenoe, David. "On the Meaning of 'Urban' in Urban Studies." *Urban Affairs Quarterly* 1, no. 1 (September 1965).

Record, Wilson. "Response of Sociologists to Black Studies." *Journal of Higher Education* XLV, no. 5 (May 1974).

Rustin, Bayard. "Black Education and White Liberalism." *New Leader*, December 22, 1969.

Schudson, Michael S. "Organizing the 'Meritocracy': A History of the College Entrance Examination Board." *Harvard Educational Review* 42, no. 1 (February 1972).

Sexton, Patricia Cayo. "The Inequality Affair: A Critique of Jencks." *Social Policy*, September-October 1973, p. 59.

Starr, Roger. "The Case of the Columbia Gym" *The Public Interest*, no. 13 (Fall 1968): 105.

Useem, Michael, and Miller, S. M. "The Upper Class in Higher Educa-
  tion." *Social Policy*, January-February 1977.
Van Den Haag, Ernest. "Black Cop-out." *National Review*, August 30,
  1974.
Van Dyne, Larry. "The Free-Tuition Fight Is Lost." *Chronicle of Higher
  Education*, September 20, 1976.
Vandevelde, Kenneth J., and Miller, Jessie L. "The Urban Grant Uni-
  versity Concept: A Systems Analysis." *Behavioral Sciences* 20, no.
  5 (September 1975).
Walker, S. Jay. "Black Studies: Phase Two." *American Scholar*, Au-
  tumn 1973.
Williams, Robert. "What We Are Learning from Current Programs for
  Disadvantaged Students." *Journal of Higher Education*, April 1969.
Wilson, Record. "Responses of Sociologists to Black Studies." *Journal
  of Higher Education* XLV, no. 5 (May 1974).
Witmer, David R. "Is the Value of College Going Really Declining?"
  Change, December 1976.
Wolin, Sheldon, and Schaar, John. "Berkeley: The Battle of People's
  Park." *New York Review of Books*, June 19, 1969.

NEWSPAPERS, NEWSMAGAZINES, AND NEWSLETTERS

Communication, March, May-June, and September 1976.
Chronicle of Higher Education, May 10, 1976; and September 20, 1976.
Long Island Press, June 1, 1969; and August 16, 1976.
Newsweek, June 9, 1969; August 11, 1969; March 18, 1974; and April
  23, 1976.
New York Times, May 26, 1969; January 23, 1970; August 30, 1970;
  May 16, 1976; June 9, 1976; October 21, 1976; October 29, 1976;
  January 17, 1977; June 19, 1977; and June 21, 1977.
Parade, August 8, 1976.
Saturday Review, June 21, 1969.
Village Voice, June 27, 1977.

BOOK REVIEWS

Fox, Richard W. Review of *The Golden Door*, by Thomas Kessner. In
  Chronicle of Higher Education, May 23, 1977, p. 12.
Wade, Richard. Review of *The Unheavenly City*, by Edward Banfield.
  Washington Post, April 26, 1970, p. 4.

INTERVIEWS

Blake, Elias, director, Institute for Service to Education, Washington,
D.C.   Interview, June 13, 1977 (Phone).

Harrison, Jim, executive director, Committee of Urban Program Universities, Washington, D.C.   Interview, June 20, 1977 (Phone).

Mallan, John, Urban Institute, Washington, D.C.   Interview, March 13, 1970 (Phone).

Maxwell, Dr. Bertha, National Council for Black Studies, Charlotte, North Carolina.   Interview, May 23, 1977 (Phone).

Sullivan, Jack, City University of New York, New York City.   Interview, May 24, 1977 (Phone).

Watson, David, Fairleigh Dickinson University, Rutherford, N.J.   Interview, October 22, 1976.

PUBLIC DOCUMENTS

Public Law 90-575, 90th Cong., S.3769, Amend. 1968. Higher Education Act of 1965.

Index

About the Author

Maurice R. Berube, an educational consultant, is the coauthor of *Local Control in Education* and *School Boards and School Policy* and coeditor of *Confrontation at Ocean Hill-Brownsville*. His articles have been published in several anthologies and in *Social Policy, Commonweal, The Nation, New Politics, Crosscurrents, The Progressive,* and other journals.